ACHIEVE LEVEL 4

MATHEMATICS
Practice Questions

By **Mark Patmore**

RISING★STARS

Rising Stars UK Ltd., 76 Farnaby Road, Bromley, BR1 4BH

www.risingstars-uk.com

Every effort has been made to trace copyright holders and obtain their permission for the use of copyright material. The authors and publishers will gladly receive information enabling them to rectify any error or omission in subsequent editions.

All facts are correct at time of going to press.

Published 2003
New Edition 2003

Text, design and layout © Rising Stars UK Ltd.

Editorial: Tanya Solomons
Design: Ken Vail Graphic Design
Layout: Fakenham Photosetting Ltd
Cover design: Burville Riley
Illustrations: Burville Riley; Beehive illustration (Theresa Tibbetts); Graham-Cameron Illustration (Tony Maher) and Jim Eldridge

All rights reserved. No part of this publication may be reproduced, stored in a retrieval system, or transmitted in any form by any means, electronic, mechanical, photocopying, recording or otherwise without the prior permission of Rising Stars UK Ltd.

British Library Cataloguing in Publication Data
A CIP record for this book is available from the British Library.

ISBN 1-904591-14-0

Printed at Wyndham Gait, Grimsby, UK

Contents

How to use this book	4
The 2004 National Tests	6
Test tips and technique	8
Level 3 Sample Test	10
The Number System and Calculations	
Place value	14
Addition and subtraction	16
Decimals	18
Finding reasonable answers	20
Proportions, fractions and percentages	22
Number patterns	24
Simple formulae	26
Measures, Shape and Space	
Coordinates	28
2D and 3D shapes	30
Reflection	32
Measures	34
Perimeter and area	36
Handling Data	
Frequency tables	38
Range and mode	40
Grouping data	42
Line graphs	44
Using and Applying Mathematics	
Problem solving 1	46
Problem solving 2	50
Level 4 Sample Test	54
Answers	58

How to use this book

Level 3 Sample Test (30 minutes)

① A warm-up test, which practises all the Level 3 Tricky Bits included in the Achieve Level 4 Maths revision book.

② Each question has space for the answers, a specific number of marks (like a real SATs question) and answers are included at the back of the book.

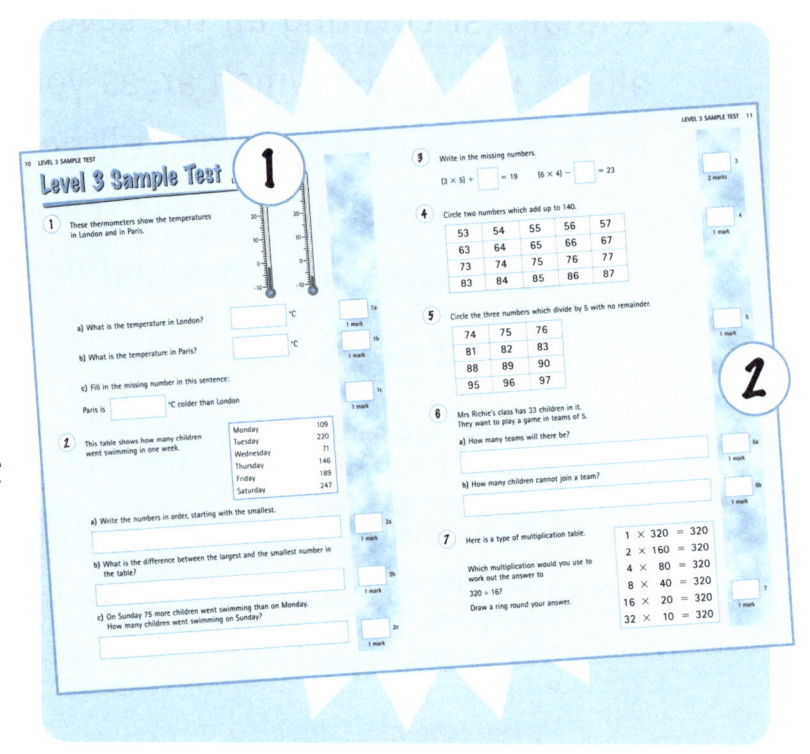

Topic questions

① A series of questions on all the topics you need to cover for the Maths Test, including some questions on Using and Applying Mathematics.

② Each question has space for the answers, a specific number of marks (like a real SATs question) and answers are included at the back of the book.

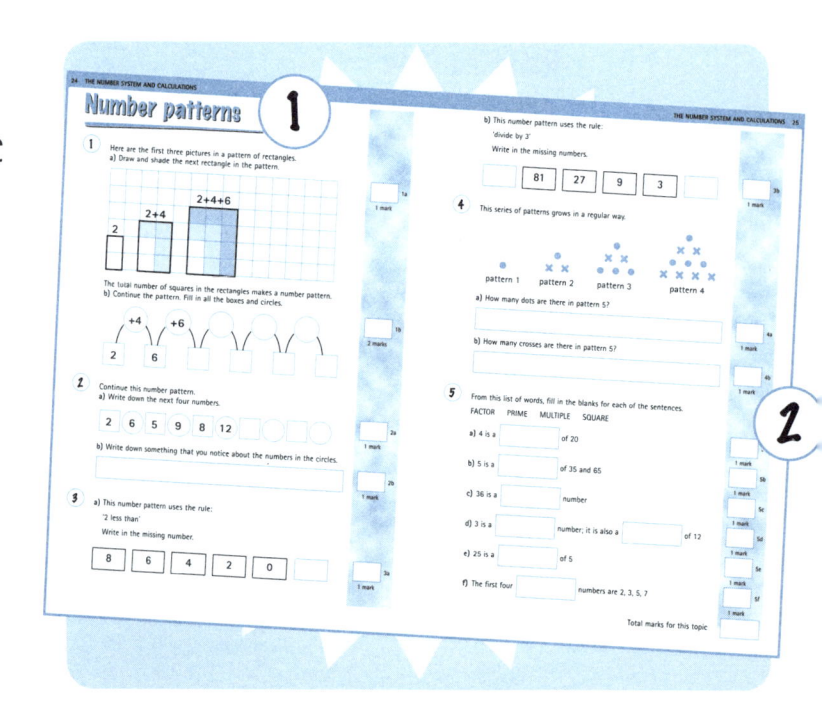

Level 4 Sample Test (45 minutes)

1) A final test covering all the Level 4 content, which allows you to see which areas you have got to grips with and which areas you still need to revise. The Sample Test is similar to the real SATs, as it starts with some easy questions and gets harder as the test goes on.

2) Each question has space for the answers, a specific number of marks (like a real SATs question) and answers are included at the back of the book.

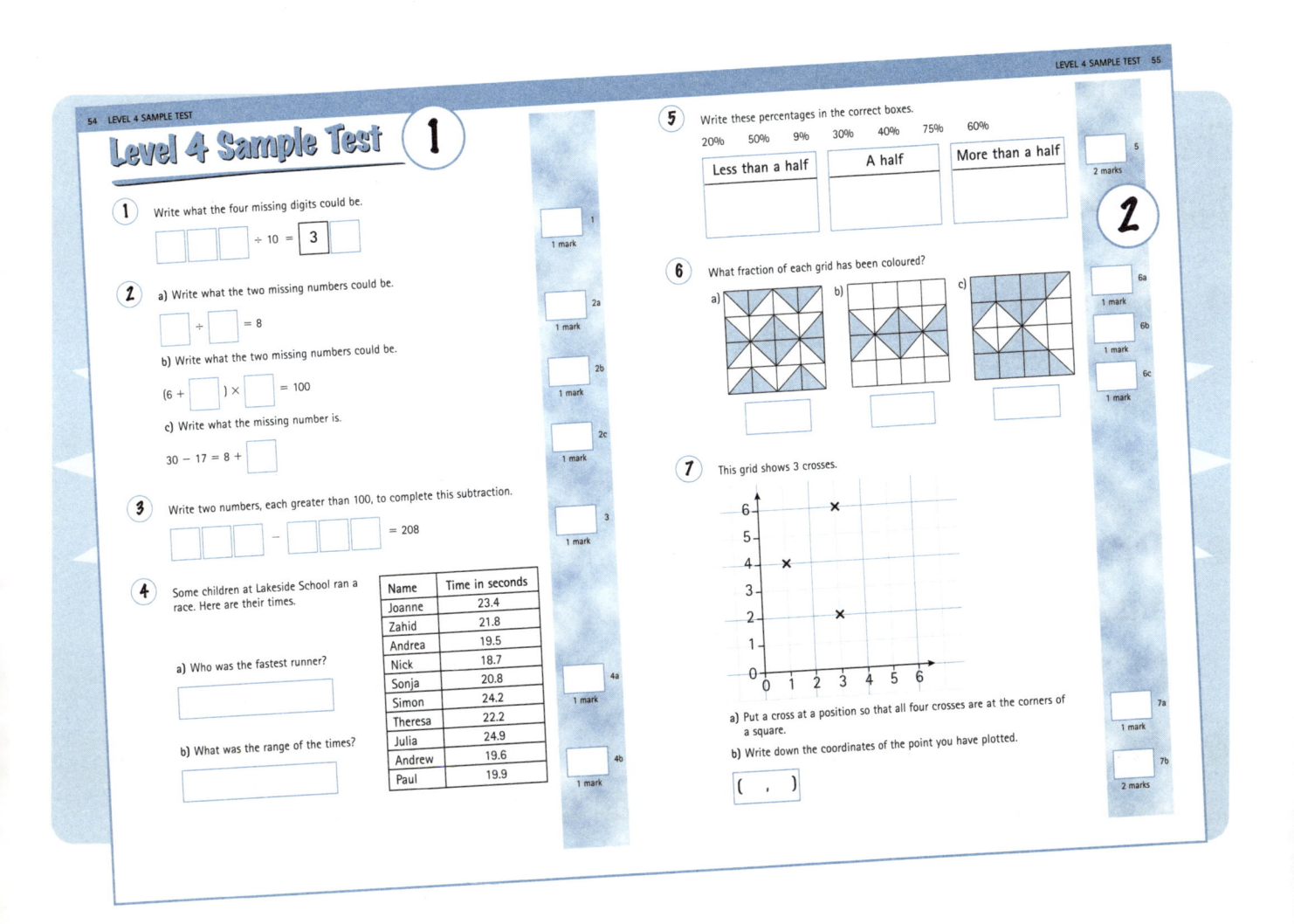

The 2004 National Tests

Key Facts

★ The Key Stage 2 National Tests (or SATs) take place in the middle of May in Year 6. You will be tested on Maths, English and Science.

★ The tests take place in your school and will be marked by examiners – not your teacher!

★ You will get your results in July, two months after you take the tests.

★ Individual test scores are not made public but a school's combined scores are published in what are commonly known as league tables.

The Maths National Tests

You will take three tests in Maths:

- **Mental Maths Test** – This test will be played to you on a cassette. You will have to answer the questions mentally within 5, 10 or 15 seconds. This test will take about 20 minutes.

- **Test A** – The non-calculator test. This test requires quick answers on a test paper. You will not be able to use a calculator but should show any working you do.

- **Test B** – This test allows you to use a calculator and includes problems that will take you longer to solve.

Using and Applying Mathematics

There will be more questions than in previous years testing how you use and apply your mathematical knowledge in different situations. This includes knowing what is the important information in the questions, how to check your results, describing things mathematically using common symbols and diagrams, and explaining your reasons for conclusions that you make.

Much of the book is written to help you get into practice for these questions. It is also worth looking at pages 46–53, which should help you with this area of Maths.

You might be asked to explain your answers and also write possible answers. Remember to always show your method.

ACHIEVE LEVEL 4

Test tips and technique

Before the test

① When you revise, try revising a 'little and often' rather than in long sessions.

② Learn your multiplication facts up to 10 × 10 so that you can recall them instantly. These are your tools for performing your calculations.

③ Revise with a friend. You can encourage and learn from each other.

④ Get a good night's sleep the night before.

⑤ Make sure you have breakfast!

⑥ Be prepared – bring your own pens and pencils and wear a watch to check the time as you go.

During the test

① Don't rush the first few questions. These tend to be quite straightforward, so don't make any silly mistakes.

② As you know by now, READ THE QUESTION THEN READ IT AGAIN.

③ If you get stuck, don't linger on the same question – move on! You can come back to it later.

④ Never leave a multiple choice question. Guess if you really can't work out the answer.

⑤ Check to see how many marks a question is worth. Have you 'earned' those marks with your answer?

⑥ Check your answers after each question. You can use the inverse method or the rounding method. Does your answer look correct?

7. Be aware of the time. After 20 minutes, check to see how far you have got.

8. Try to leave a couple of minutes at the end to read through what you have written.

9. Always show your method. You may get a mark for showing you have gone through the correct procedure even if your answer is wrong.

10. Don't leave any questions unanswered. In the two minutes you have left yourself at the end, make an educated guess at the questions you really couldn't do.

11. Remember, as long as you have done your best, nobody can ask for more. Only you will know if that is the case.

Things to remember

1. Don't panic! If you see a difficult question, take your time, re-read it and have a go!

2. Check every question and every page to be sure you don't miss any! Some questions will want two answers.

3. If a question is about measuring, always write in the UNIT of MEASUREMENT (e.g. cm, l, kg).

4. Don't be afraid to ask a teacher for anything you need, such as tracing paper or a protractor.

5. Write neatly – if you want to change an answer, put a line through it and write beside the answer box.

6. Always double-check your answers.

Good luck!

Level 3 Sample Test

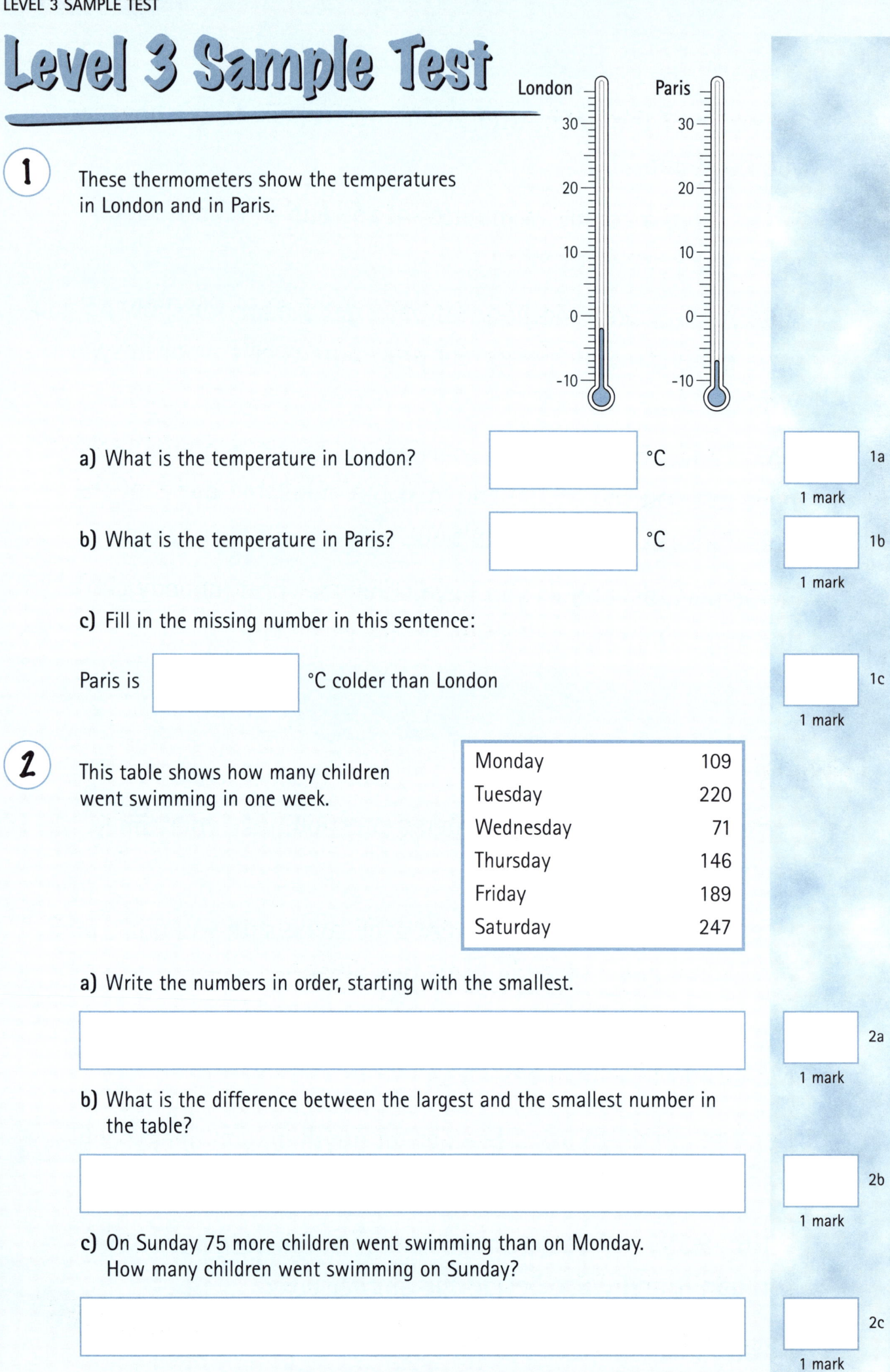

1 These thermometers show the temperatures in London and in Paris.

London / Paris thermometers

a) What is the temperature in London? ☐ °C — 1 mark (1a)

b) What is the temperature in Paris? ☐ °C — 1 mark (1b)

c) Fill in the missing number in this sentence:

Paris is ☐ °C colder than London — 1 mark (1c)

2 This table shows how many children went swimming in one week.

Monday	109
Tuesday	220
Wednesday	71
Thursday	146
Friday	189
Saturday	247

a) Write the numbers in order, starting with the smallest.

☐ — 1 mark (2a)

b) What is the difference between the largest and the smallest number in the table?

☐ — 1 mark (2b)

c) On Sunday 75 more children went swimming than on Monday. How many children went swimming on Sunday?

☐ — 1 mark (2c)

3 Write in the missing numbers.

(3 × 5) + ☐ = 19   (6 × 4) − ☐ = 23

3

2 marks

4 Circle two numbers which add up to 140.

53	54	55	56	57
63	64	65	66	67
73	74	75	76	77
83	84	85	86	87

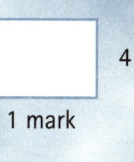

4

1 mark

5 Circle the three numbers which divide by 5 with no remainder.

74	75	76
81	82	83
88	89	90
95	96	97

5

1 mark

6 Mrs Richie's class has 33 children in it.
They want to play a game in teams of 5.

a) How many teams will there be?

6a

1 mark

b) How many children cannot join a team?

6b

1 mark

7 Here is a type of multiplication table.

Which multiplication would you use to work out the answer to

320 ÷ 16?

Draw a ring round your answer.

| 1 × 320 = 320 |
| 2 × 160 = 320 |
| 4 × 80 = 320 |
| 8 × 40 = 320 |
| 16 × 20 = 320 |
| 32 × 10 = 320 |

7

1 mark

LEVEL 3 SAMPLE TEST   11

8 Look at these shapes.

a) Which shapes have one line of symmetry?

b) Which shapes have more than one line of symmetry?

c) Which shapes have no lines of symmetry?

9 This pictogram shows the number of comics some children in class 6 had.

Number of comics

Ann	
Paul	
David	
Jane	
Robert	35

represents 10 comics   represents 5 comics

a) Show the number of comics each child has in the last column.

b) Complete the pictogram showing the number of comics Robert has.

10 Draw one line to join two fractions which have the same value.

$$\frac{4}{7}$$

$$\frac{1}{2}$$ $$\frac{2}{8}$$

$$\frac{2}{5}$$ $$\frac{1}{3}$$

$$\frac{1}{4}$$

1 mark

11 On this grid shade in 6 small squares.

What fraction of the grid have you shaded in? ▢/▢

Show another way of writing this fraction. ▢/▢

2 marks

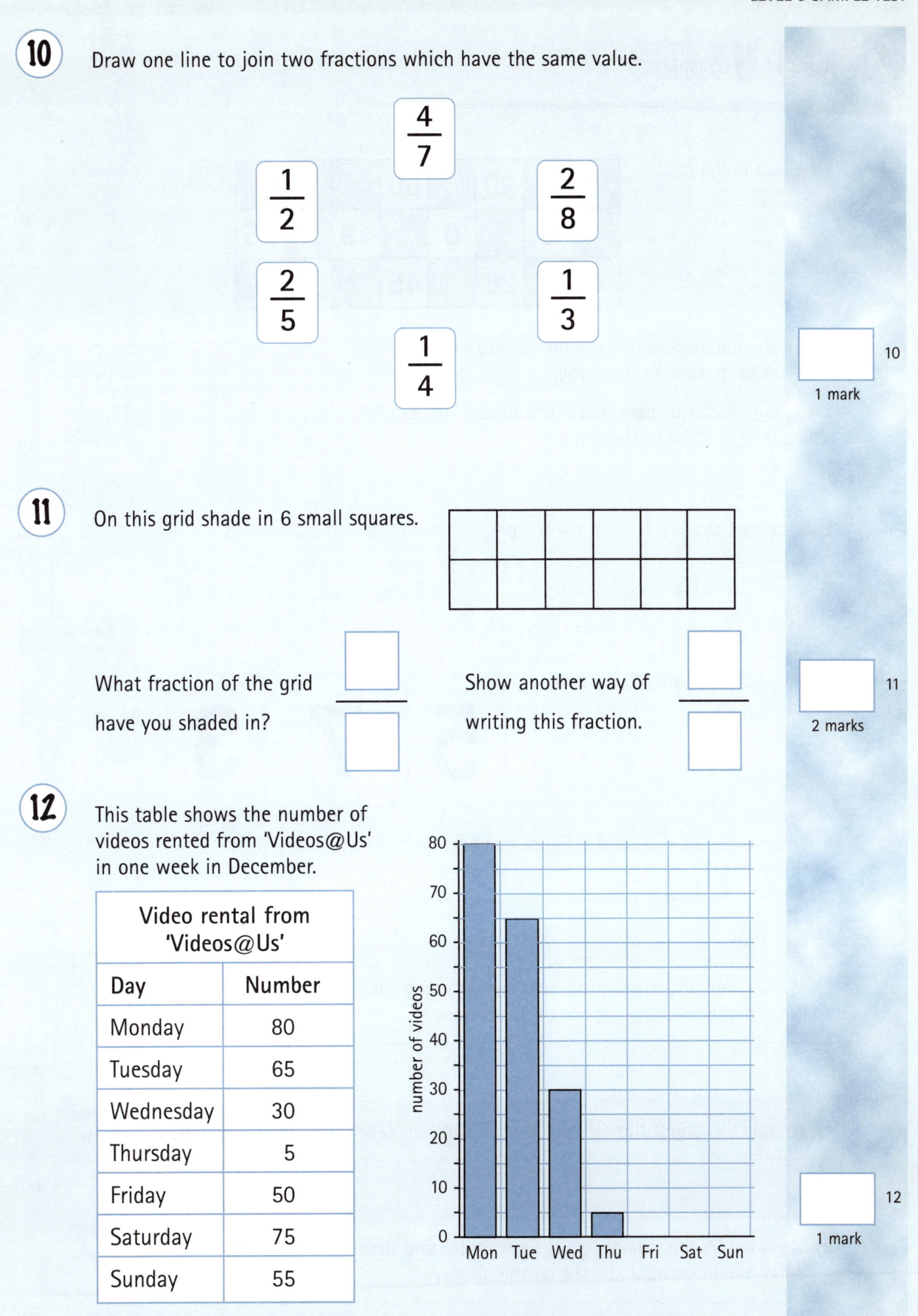

12 This table shows the number of videos rented from 'Videos@Us' in one week in December.

| Video rental from 'Videos@Us' ||
Day	Number
Monday	80
Tuesday	65
Wednesday	30
Thursday	5
Friday	50
Saturday	75
Sunday	55

Complete the bar chart showing the number rented on Friday, Saturday and Sunday.

1 mark

Total marks for the test ▢/22

Place value

14 THE NUMBER SYSTEM AND CALCULATIONS

1 Here is a Bingo card.

	20		30			
	9		6		19	25
4		26		45		2

Circle the numbers that 2 will divide into exactly.
One has been done to show you.

Cross out those numbers that 5 will divide into exactly.
One has been done to show you.

2 marks

2 Use the fact that 19 × 6 = 114 to complete the following statements:

6 × ☐ = 114   114 ÷ ☐ = 19   ☐ ÷ 6 = 38

3 marks

3 Molly has three cards. Each card has a digit on it.

5 7 3

a) What is the smallest three-figure number she can make using the three cards?

1 mark

b) Molly enters this number on her calculator and then multiplies it by 10. What number should she see on the display?

1 mark

c) What is the largest three-figure number she can make using the three cards?

1 mark

d) Molly enters this number on her calculator and then divides it by 3. What number should she see on the display?

1 mark

THE NUMBER SYSTEM AND CALCULATIONS 15

4 Here is a division grid:

÷	2	3	4
36	18	12	9
12	6	4	3
24	12	8	6

Make sure you understand how it works. For example, it shows that 36 ÷ 4 is 9, or that 24 ÷ 3 is 8.

Complete the following division grid:

÷	2	3	6
30	15		
48	24	16	
18		6	

4
2 marks

5 a) Circle the correct answer.

170 units is the same as

17 hundreds   17 tens   170 tens

5a
1 mark

b) Put a ring round the number which is 10 times 120.

1020   2100   1002   1200   2010

5b
1 mark

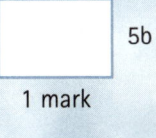

6 Write in the missing digit.

```
    5 □
  ×   8
  ─────
  4 5 6
```

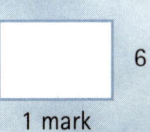

6
1 mark

Total marks for this topic

Addition and subtraction

1 In this list some pairs of numbers add up to 1000, some pairs add up to 2000 and some add up to 5000.

462	856	3836	262
819	1144	959	658
1254	1164	191	1074
2646	4041	929	738
538	3746	1342	2354

a) Write down a pair of numbers that add up to 1000.

☐ and ☐ *1a, 1 mark*

b) Write down a pair of numbers that add up to 2000.

☐ and ☐ *1b, 1 mark*

c) Write down a pair of numbers that add up to 5000.

☐ and ☐ *1c, 1 mark*

2 Fill in the missing numbers in the boxes.

(☐ × 6) ÷ 3 = 12

5 × (8 ÷ ☐) = 20

2, 2 marks

3 Write in the missing digits.

```
    2 ☐ 8
+   2 9 ☐
  -------
    5 5 5
```

3, 1 mark

THE NUMBER SYSTEM AND CALCULATIONS   17

4 Write in the missing digit.
The answer does not have a remainder.

$$3 \overline{) \fbox{} 8 } \text{ gives } 26$$

4
1 mark

5 Bold Lane car park has 5 levels and 600 parking spaces.
This table shows how many cars were in the car park one Saturday morning.

Level	Number of cars
1	99
2	115
3	78
4	120
5	106

How many parking spaces were left?

5
1 mark

6 Write the missing numbers in the circles using these rules.

For ↗ you multiply by 10
For ↖ you multiply by 5
For → you multiply by 2

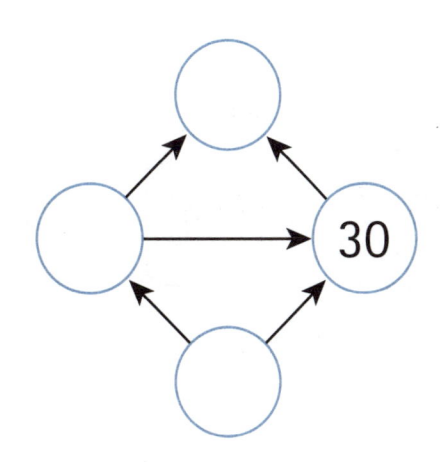

6
1 mark

Total marks for this topic

Decimals

1) One length of a swimming pool is 25 metres.
a) How many lengths are there in a 150 metre race?

Six children swim a 50 metre race.

Lane	Name	Time in seconds
1	Thomas	89.2
2	Peter	86.3
3	Kathy	84.7
4	Nisha	92.4
5	Jodie	85.1
6	Helen	90.4

b) Who finished first?

c) How many seconds faster than Thomas was Peter?

2) These tins show the amounts collected for a charity.

£3.55   £8.67   £7.56   £11.32   £9.65

What was the total amount collected?

3 In this chart any three numbers in a line, across or down, have a total of 15.45.
Write the missing number.

1.46	7.61	6.38
10.07		0.23
3.92	2.69	8.84

3
1 mark

4 Match these addition and subtraction questions to their correct answers.
The first one has been done for you.

1.39 + 3.21 → 4.60

3.21 − 1.10   9.11

6.01 + 3.10   9.99

9.01 − 8.75   2.11

6.88 − 5.19   0.26

8.80 + 1.19   1.69

4
2 marks

5 a) Write the next three numbers in this series:

6.04, 6.03, 6.02, ☐ , ☐ , ☐

5a
1 mark

b) Put these numbers in order from the smallest to the largest:

2.26   1.85   2.9   1.35   0.64   0.621

5b
1 mark

Total marks for this topic

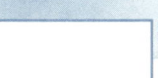

Finding reasonable answers

1 Ben and Annie are raising money. They take part in a sponsored walk.

a) Ben was promised 90p for every kilometre he walked. How much money did Ben collect if he walked 11 km?

1a
1 mark

b) Annie walked 13 km. She collected 80p for each kilometre she walked. How much did she collect?

1b
1 mark

Annie's mother said:
Tell me how much you collected for your walk and I will give a quarter of that amount.

c) How much should Annie's mother give her?

1c
1 mark

d) How could Annie check that the amount was right?

1d
1 mark

2 This picture shows a new football stand.
It has 18 rows of 157 seats.

a) How many people can sit in the stand?

2a
2 marks

b) How could you check your calculation to see if your answer is right?

2b
2 marks

THE NUMBER SYSTEM AND CALCULATIONS 21

3 Write each of these numbers to the nearest whole number.

a) 14.7 is nearest to [ ]

3a [ ] 1 mark

b) $5\frac{3}{8}$ is nearest to [ ]

3b [ ] 1 mark

c) 6.38 is nearest to [ ]

3c [ ] 1 mark

4 Mrs Bates is planning the school trip.
200 children and 15 adults are going to the seaside by coach.
Each coach can carry 60 people.
How many coaches should Mrs Bates order?

[ ]

4 [ ] 2 marks

5 Some children from Stayton School go camping.
The cost for 6 nights is £22 for each child.

a) What does it cost for 1 night?
Give your answer to the nearest pence.

[ ]

5a [ ] 2 marks

b) 70 children go camping. Each tent takes up to 6 children.
What is the least number of tents they will need?

[ ]

5b [ ] 2 marks

6 Simon goes shopping. Here is his list:

Flour	1.5 kg
Tin of potatoes	800 g
Tin of beans	420 g

a) Simon estimates that the weight of the shopping will be about 1200 g.
How do you know he must be wrong?

[ ]

6a [ ] 2 marks

b) Calculate the correct weight of the shopping.

[ ]

6b [ ] 2 marks

Total marks for this topic [ ]

Proportions, fractions and percentages

1 Write down the answers to the following calculations:

a) $\frac{2}{5}$ of £2.50 = £ ☐

b) $\frac{3}{4}$ of £4.80 = £ ☐

c) $\frac{3}{10}$ of 2 litres = ☐ millilitres

2 What fraction of these shapes is shaded?

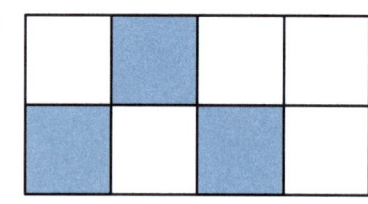

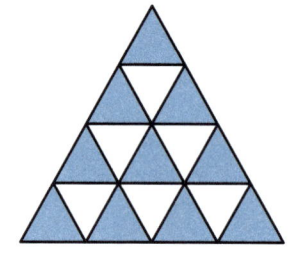

a)

b)

3 This 6 × 10 grid is made of centimetre squares.
Part of the grid has been coloured.

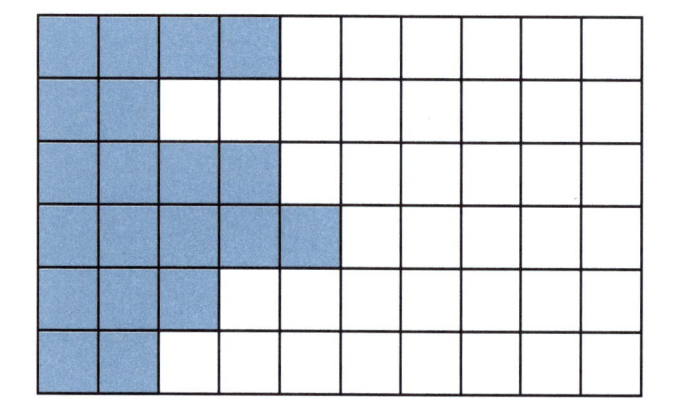

a) What fraction of the grid has not been coloured?

THE NUMBER SYSTEM AND CALCULATIONS 23

b) How many squares are there in 25% of the whole grid?

3b
1 mark

4 $\frac{2}{4}$ and $\frac{4}{8}$ are fractions equal to $\frac{1}{2}$

a) Write down another fraction equal to $\frac{1}{2}$

4a
1 mark

$\frac{2}{6}$ and $\frac{4}{12}$ are fractions equal to $\frac{1}{3}$

b) Write down another fraction equal to $\frac{1}{3}$

4b
1 mark

5 David and Mary played a game with some fraction cards.

$\frac{1}{10}$ $\frac{1}{3}$ $\frac{1}{20}$ $\frac{2}{8}$ $\frac{6}{10}$

$\frac{1}{100}$ $\frac{60}{100}$ $\frac{25}{50}$ $\frac{3}{5}$ $\frac{4}{8}$

They decided to sort the cards into three groups.
Write which fraction they should place in each group.

Less than a half	A half	More than a half

5
3 marks

Total marks for this topic

Number patterns

1) Here are the first three pictures in a pattern of rectangles.
a) Draw and shade the next rectangle in the pattern.

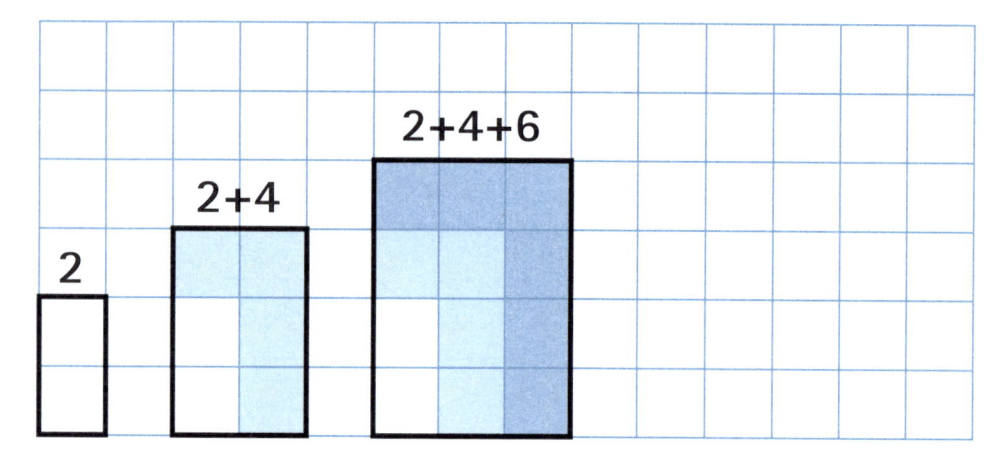

2 | 2+4 | 2+4+6

The total number of squares in the rectangles makes a number pattern.
b) Continue the pattern. Fill in all the boxes and circles.

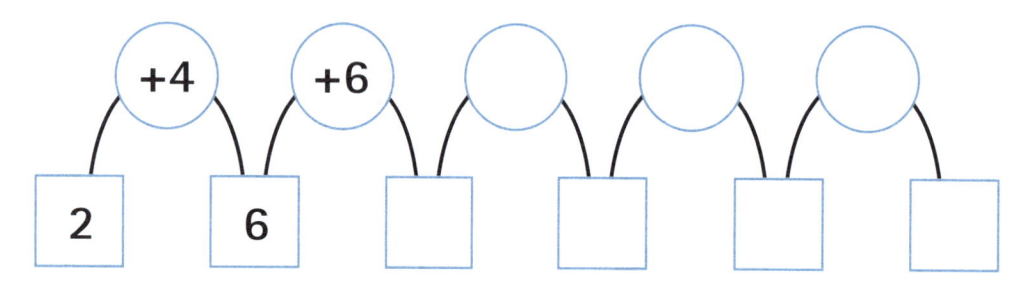

2 →(+4)→ 6 →(+6)→ ☐ →( )→ ☐ →( )→ ☐ →( )→ ☐

1a — 1 mark
1b — 2 marks

2) Continue this number pattern.
a) Write down the next four numbers.

| 2 | (6) | 5 | (9) | 8 | (12) | ☐ | ( ) | ☐ | ( ) |

b) Write down something that you notice about the numbers in the circles.

2a — 1 mark
2b — 1 mark

3) a) This number pattern uses the rule:

'2 less than'

Write in the missing number.

| 8 | 6 | 4 | 2 | 0 | ☐ |

3a — 1 mark

b) This number pattern uses the rule:

'divide by 3'

Write in the missing numbers.

| | 81 | 27 | 9 | 3 | |

3b
1 mark

4 This series of patterns grows in a regular way.

pattern 1   pattern 2   pattern 3   pattern 4

a) How many dots are there in pattern 5?

4a
1 mark

b) How many crosses are there in pattern 5?

4b
1 mark

5 From this list of words, fill in the blanks for each of the sentences.

FACTOR   PRIME   MULTIPLE   SQUARE

a) 4 is a _____ of 20

5a
1 mark

b) 5 is a _____ of 35 and 65

5b
1 mark

c) 36 is a _____ number

5c
1 mark

d) 3 is a _____ number; it is also a _____ of 12

5d
1 mark

e) 25 is a _____ of 5

5e
1 mark

f) The first four _____ numbers are 2, 3, 5, 7

5f
1 mark

Total marks for this topic

Simple formulae

1 Lottie would like a bouncy castle at her birthday party.
The cost of hiring the castle is worked out using the formula:

Cost in £ = 12 × number of hours hired + 15

Find the cost of hiring the castle for 4 hours.

2 marks

2 Harry has found a rule to calculate the speed of a car.
The rule is:

> Count the number of seconds it takes to pass between two lamp posts.
> Divide 75 by this number.
> The answer is the speed of the car in miles per hour.

A car takes 3 seconds to pass between two lamp posts.
Use Harry's rule to find the speed of the car.

2 marks

3 Robert and Robin used a 45 degree right-angled triangle to measure the height of a tower.
This is how they did it:

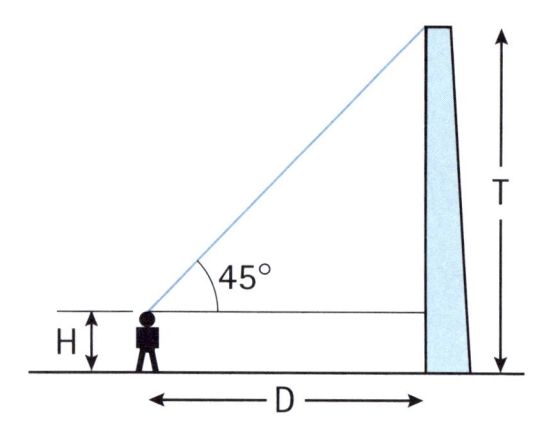

Robin said:

'The height of the tower (T), is equal to the sum of the distance of Robert from the tower, (D) and Robert's height (H).'

Robert is 1.5 m tall. He stands 17 m from the tower.
Use the formula to calculate the height of the tower.

2 marks

4 This formula connects the number of crayons and the number of boxes:

> number of crayons = number of boxes × 16

a) How many crayons are there in 12 boxes?

b) How many boxes do you need for 48 crayons?

5 The cost to hire a motorbike is given by the following formula:

Cost = £3 × number of hours + £2

Fill in the missing values in the table.

Time in hours	Cost in £
1	5
4	
	17

6 James and Judy are playing a 'Think of a number' game. James' rule is:

> I think of a number, times by 2 then add 10

a) What answer does James get if the number he thinks of is 2?

Judy's rule is:

> I think of a number, times by 5 then add 1

b) Judy's answer is 41. What number did she think of?

Total marks for this topic

Coordinates

1) A straight line can be drawn through the crosses and circles on this grid.

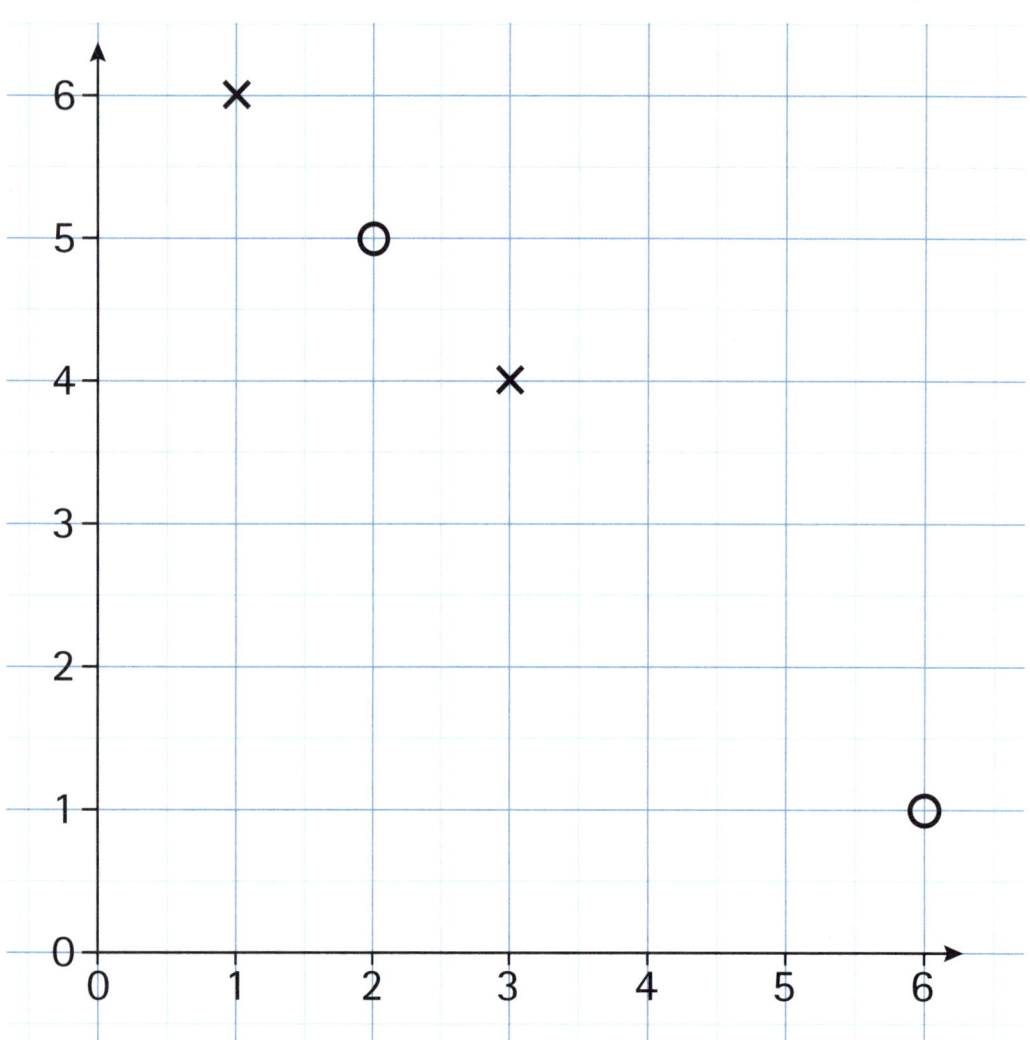

a) Put two more crosses on the grid which are in the same straight line as the other crosses and circles.

1 mark — 1a

b) Write the coordinates of the crosses and circles in order.
The first two have been done for you.

(1, 6)   (2, 5)   (,)   (,)   (,)   (,)

1 mark — 1b

c) Look at the coordinates to find any number patterns.
Write about two number patterns you have seen.

2 marks — 1c

2 Ann and Katy are playing a coordinate game.
They each call out two points which are on a straight line.
Ann calls out (5, 1) and (1, 5). Her points are shown with crosses (X).
Katy calls out (1, 3) and (5, 3). Her points are shown with circles (O).

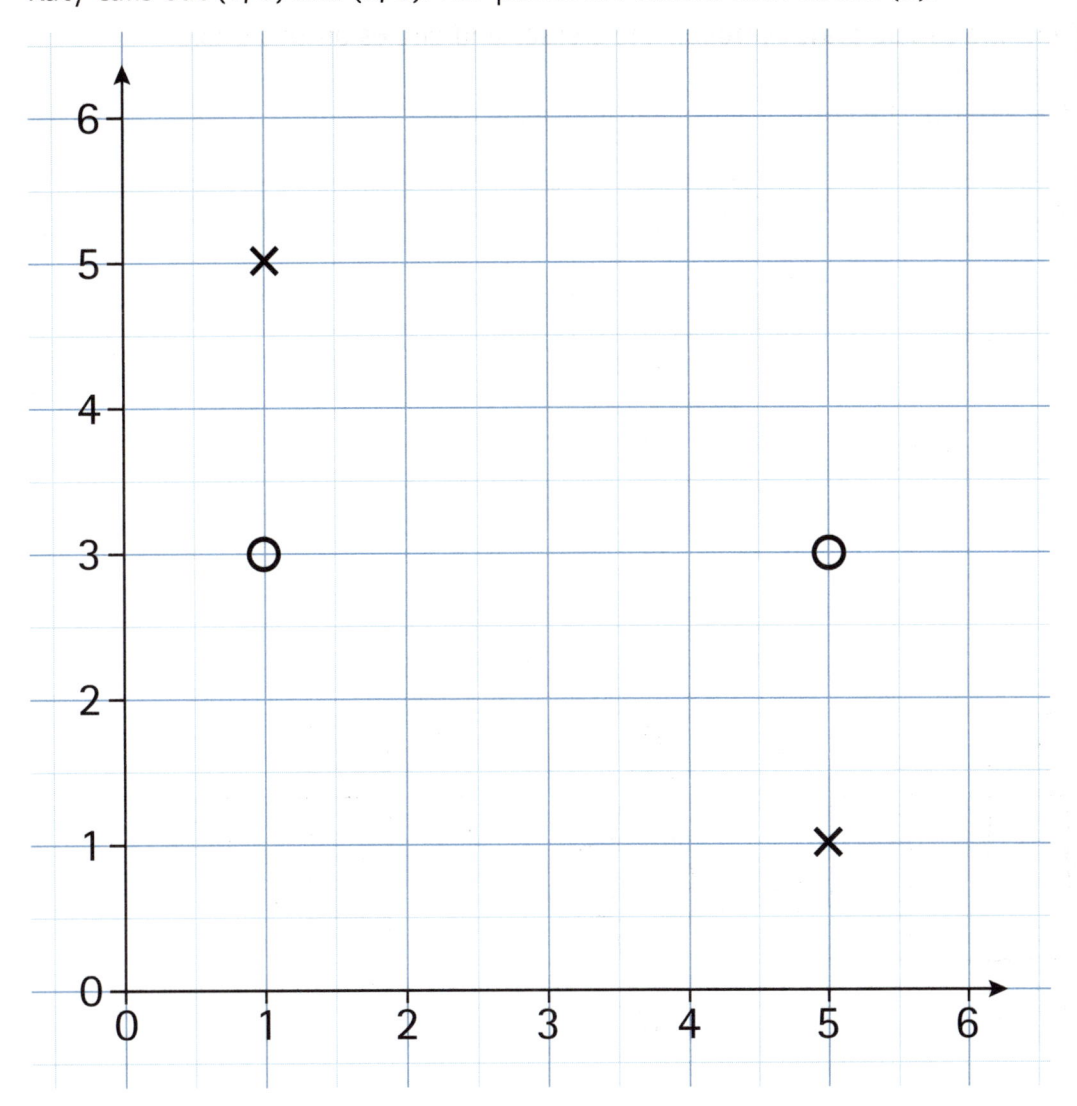

a) Plot a point which is in the same straight line as Ann's points and which will also be on the same line as Katy's points.

b) Write down the coordinates of your point.

Total marks for this topic

2D and 3D shapes

1) Here are 5 solid shapes and 5 nets.
Match each shape to its net.
Write the letter of the correct net under the shape.

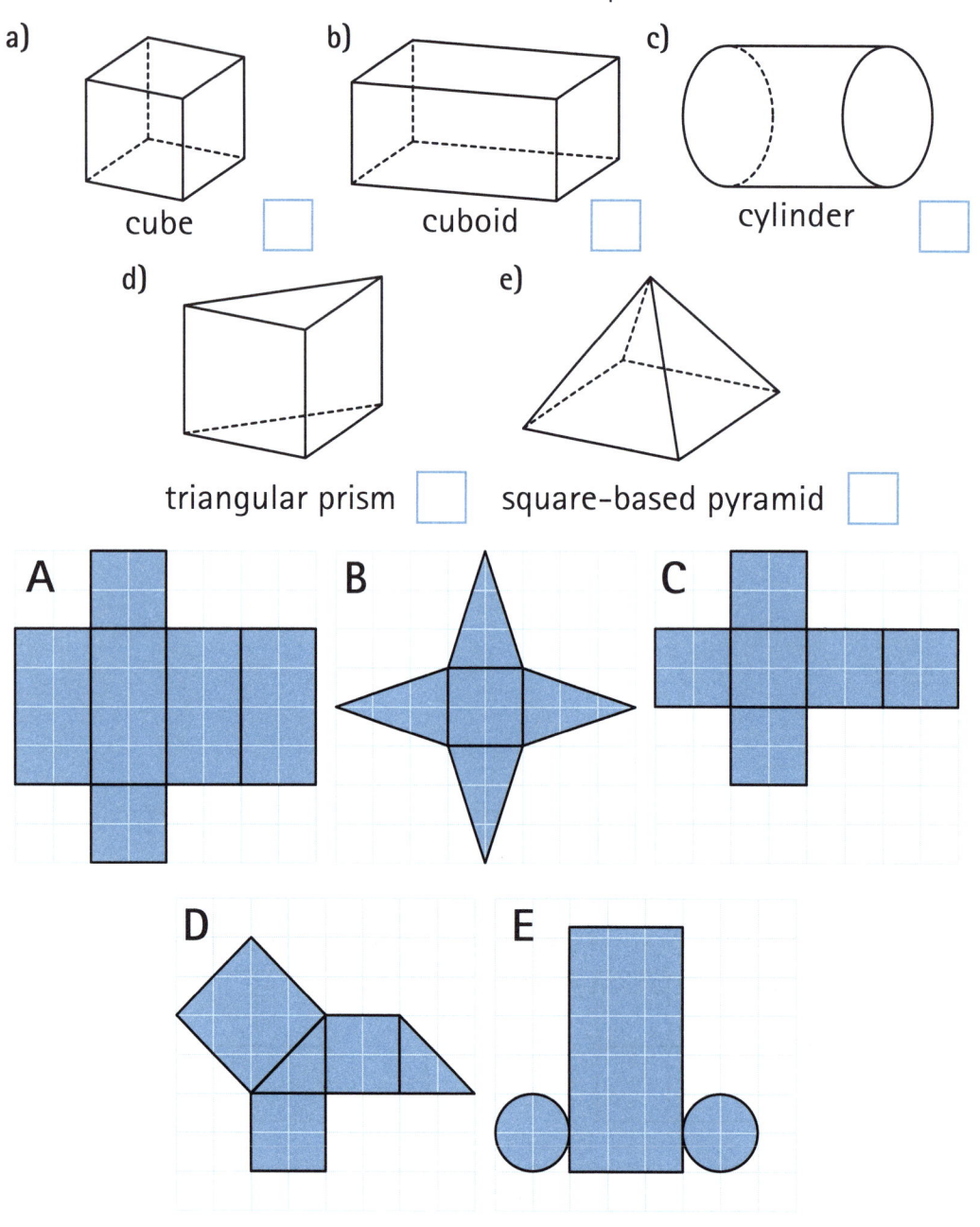

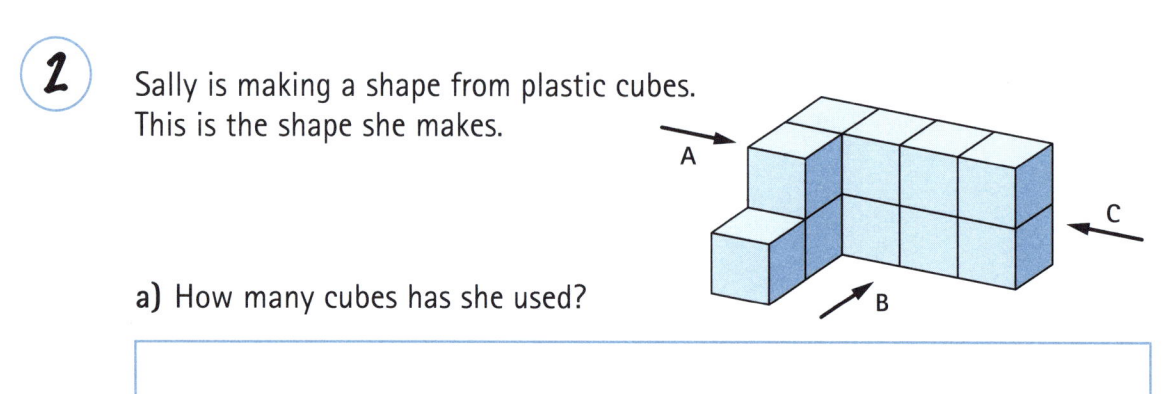

a) cube

b) cuboid

c) cylinder

d) triangular prism

e) square-based pyramid

A B C

D E

1a 1 mark
1b 1 mark
1c 1 mark
1d 1 mark
1e 1 mark

2) Sally is making a shape from plastic cubes.
This is the shape she makes.

a) How many cubes has she used?

2a 1 mark

b) Sally turns the shape around and looks at it in 3 different ways.

Here are the 3 pictures Sally will see when she looks at her shape, one when she looks at it from A, one from B and one from C.
Write underneath each picture whether it is what Sally will see from A or from B or from C.

(i) ☐   (ii) ☐   (iii) ☐

2b — 2 marks

3 **a)** On the grid below draw a triangle with 1 right angle.   **b)** On the grid below draw a quadrilateral with only 2 right angles.   **c)** On the grid below draw a pentagon with 3 right angles.

3a — 1 mark
3b — 1 mark
3c — 1 mark

4 Here are some shapes made out of centimetre squares.

A   B   C   D

a) Which ones will not fold up to make an open box?

4a — 1 mark

b) Which one does not have a perimeter of 12 cm?

4b — 1 mark

Total marks for this topic ☐

Reflection

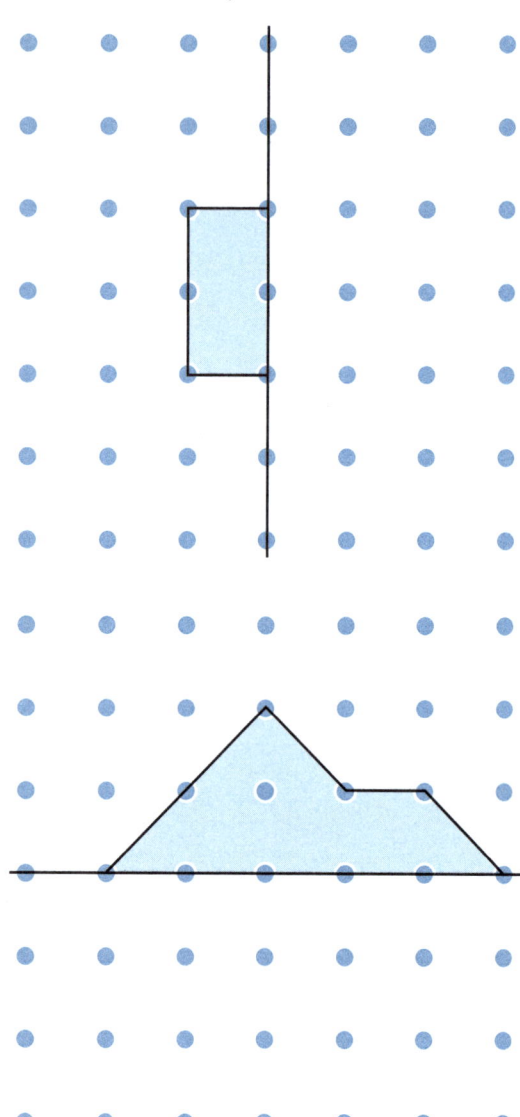

1 Reflect each shape below in the mirror line.

1a
1 mark

1b
1 mark

2 Draw the reflection of this triangle in the mirror line.

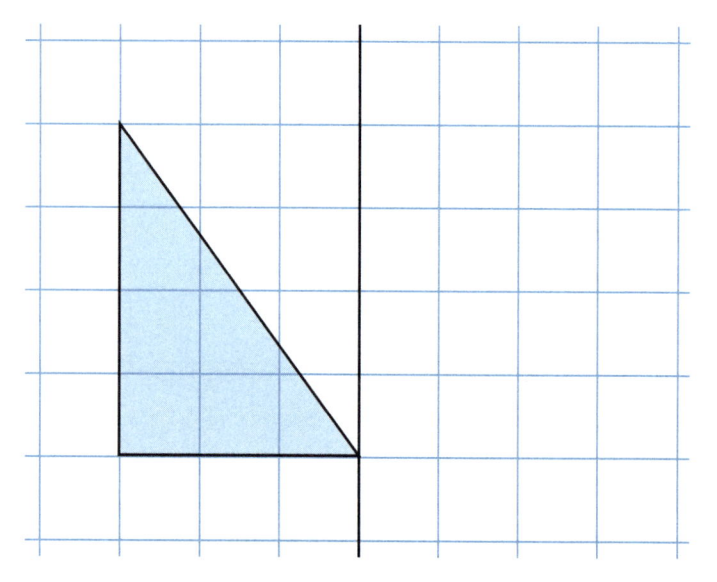

2
1 mark

MEASURES, SHAPE AND SPACE 33

3 Here are some shapes.
Reflect each one in the mirror line.

a)

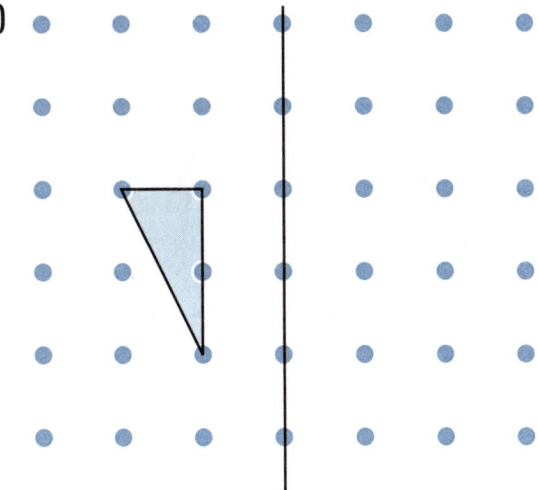

	3a
1 mark	

b)

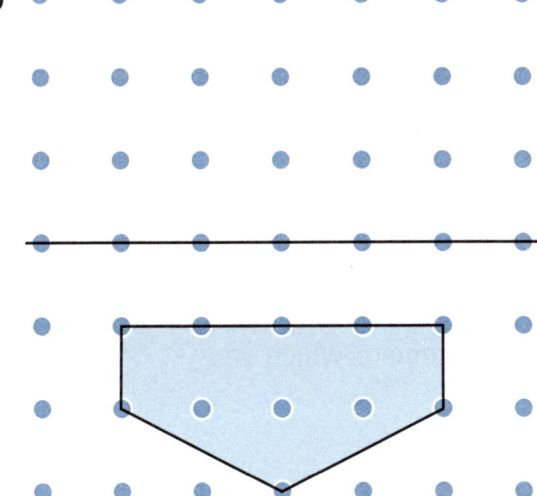

	3b
1 mark	

Total marks for this topic

Measures

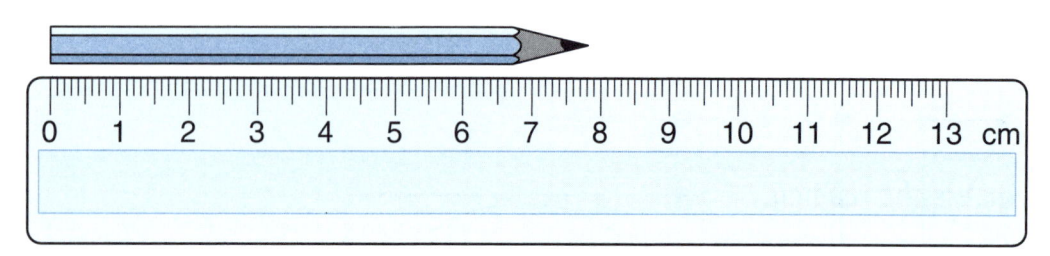

1) Here is a picture of a pencil.

What is the length of the pencil.
Give your answer in centimetres, correct to one decimal place.

[ ] 1
1 mark

2) The picture shows part of a metre rule.
Write down the values that arrows A, B and C are pointing to on this rule.

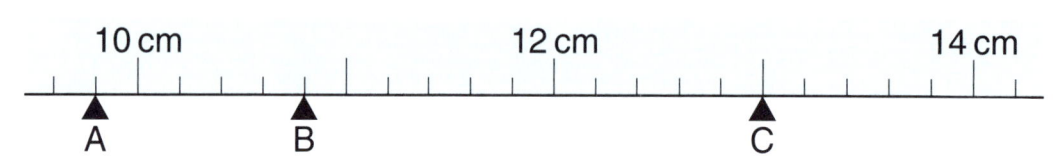

10 cm   12 cm   14 cm

A   B   C

a) A = [ ] cm   b) B = [ ] cm   c) C = [ ] cm

[ ] 2a
1 mark

[ ] 2b
1 mark

[ ] 2c
1 mark

3) For each of the following put a tick, ✔, by the statement which you think is true.

a) A glass holds 0.25 litres of water [ ]

A glass holds 2.5 litres of water [ ]

A glass holds 25 litres of water [ ]

A glass holds 250 litres of water [ ]

[ ] 3a
1 mark

b) Your foot is about 20 mm long [ ]

Your foot is about 20 cm long [ ]

Your foot is about 2 m long [ ]

Your foot is about 20 m long [ ]

[ ] 3b
1 mark

c) An apple weighs about 1 gram ☐

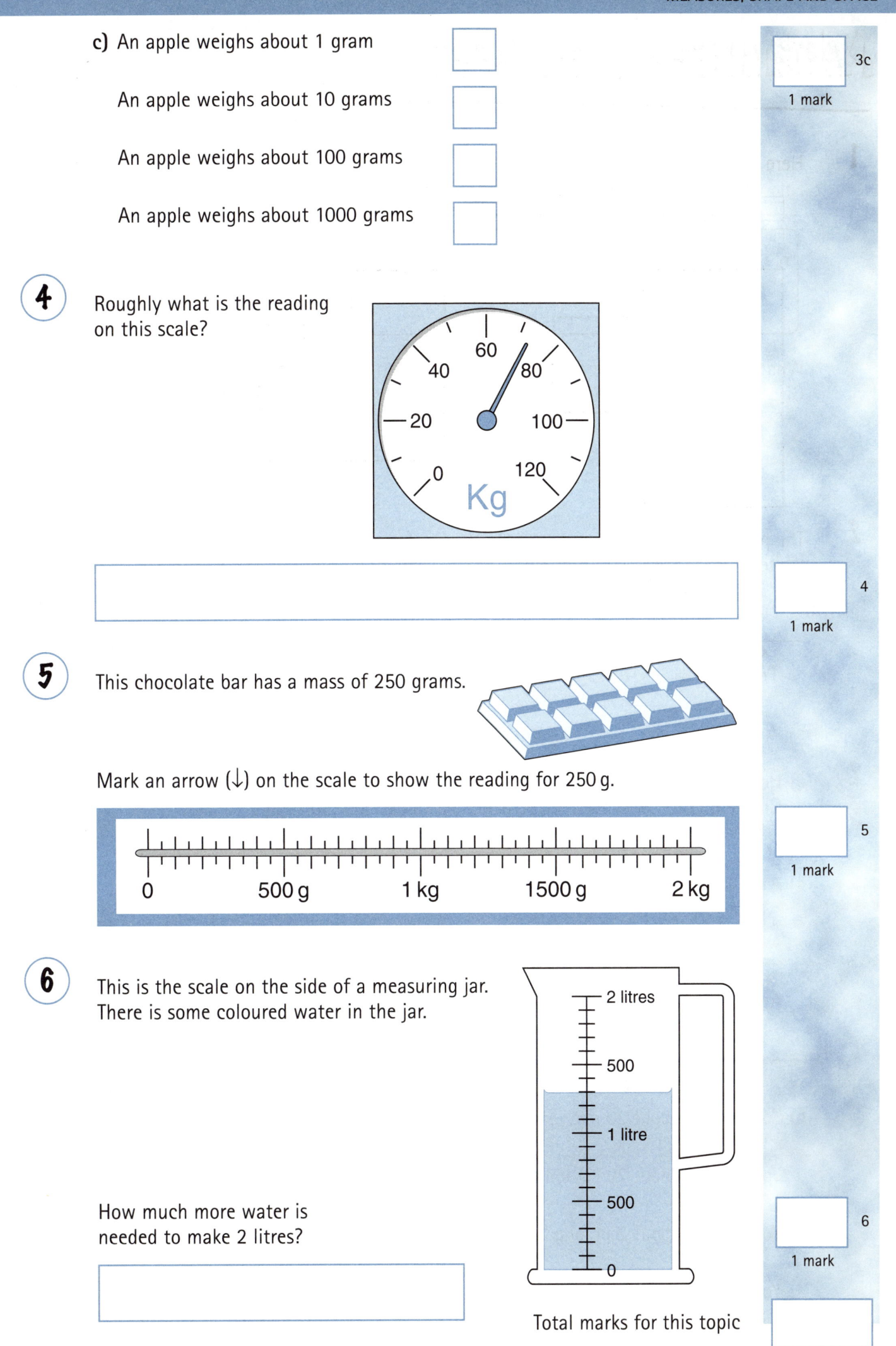

An apple weighs about 10 grams ☐

An apple weighs about 100 grams ☐

An apple weighs about 1000 grams ☐

4 Roughly what is the reading on this scale?

5 This chocolate bar has a mass of 250 grams.

Mark an arrow (↓) on the scale to show the reading for 250 g.

6 This is the scale on the side of a measuring jar. There is some coloured water in the jar.

How much more water is needed to make 2 litres?

Total marks for this topic

Perimeter and area

1 Each square represents 1 cm.
Find the area and the perimeter of these shapes.

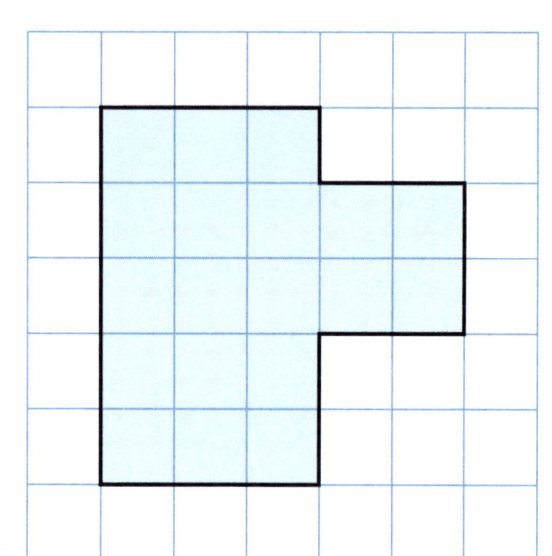

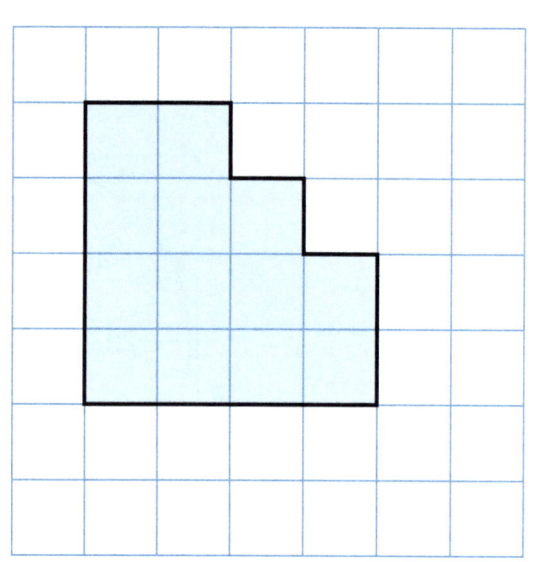

a) Area = ☐ sq cm

Perimeter = ☐ cm

b) Area = ☐ sq cm

Perimeter = ☐ cm

2 a) Here is a centimetre square grid.
On the grid below draw a shape which has an area of 10 square centimetres.

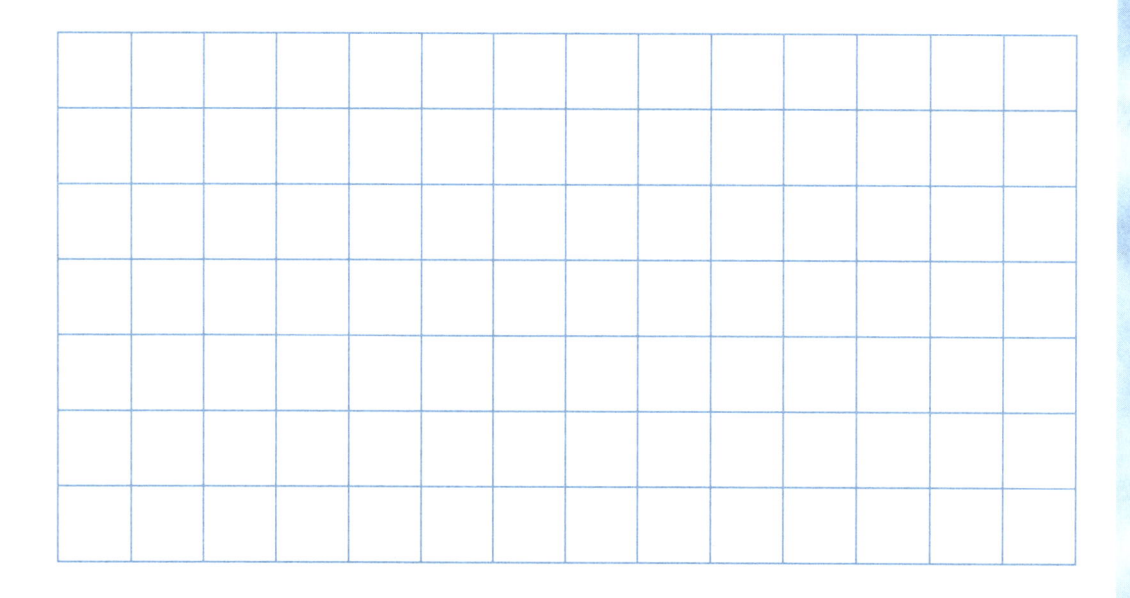

b) On the grid of centimetre squares below draw a rectangle which has a perimeter of 10 centimetres.

2b
1 mark

3 Here is a shaded shape on a grid made of centimetre squares.

a) What area is shaded?

cm²

3a
1 mark

b) What fraction of the area of the grid is shaded?

3b
1 mark

Total marks for this topic

Frequency tables

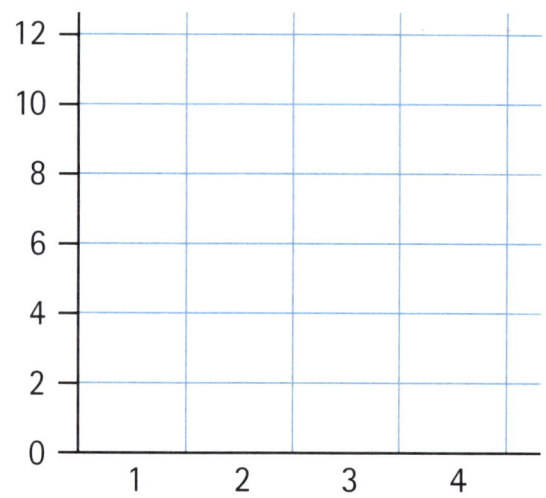

1) Mrs Khan asked the 27 pupils in her class: 'How many children are in your family?' Here are their answers:

2   2   2   1   1   3   2   2   1   1   3   4   2   1

1   2   2   1   3   3   2   2   1   1   2   1   2

Mrs Khan recorded the answers in a frequency table:

Number of children	Tally	Total
1	//// ////	10
2		
3		
4		

a) Complete the frequency table.

b) Draw a bar chart to show the results.

number of families (y-axis: 0, 2, 4, 6, 8, 10, 12)
number of children in family (x-axis: 1, 2, 3, 4)

2) Sally asked each person in her class what their shoe size was.

Here are her results:

7	5	6	8	4	5
6	7	8	7	5	6
6	5	7	6	6	8
7	5	6	6	7	7
5	6	5	5	6	7

a) Complete this frequency table.

Shoe size	Tally	Total
4	/	
5	//// ///	
6	//// ////	
7		
8		

1a 2 marks

1b 2 marks

2a 2 marks

b) Draw a bar chart to show the sizes.

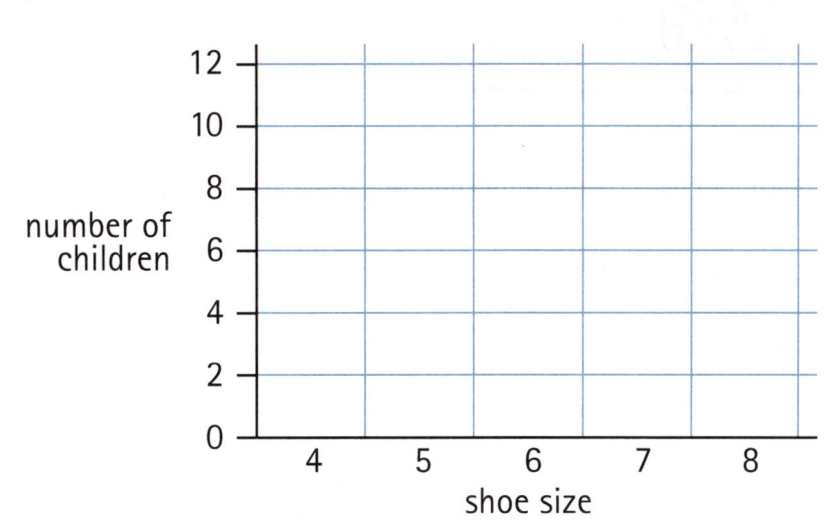

2b
2 marks

3 Jodi asked some children in her class: 'What is your favourite colour?'

She wrote down their answers:

blue; yellow; red; yellow; green; blue; blue; red; white; green; red; red; blue; yellow; green; white.

Jodi started a frequency table to show this data – she tallied all the blue ones.

a) Complete this frequency table.

Colour	Tally	Frequency
blue	////	
yellow		
red		
green		
white		

3a
2 marks

b) Complete this bar chart to show the results.

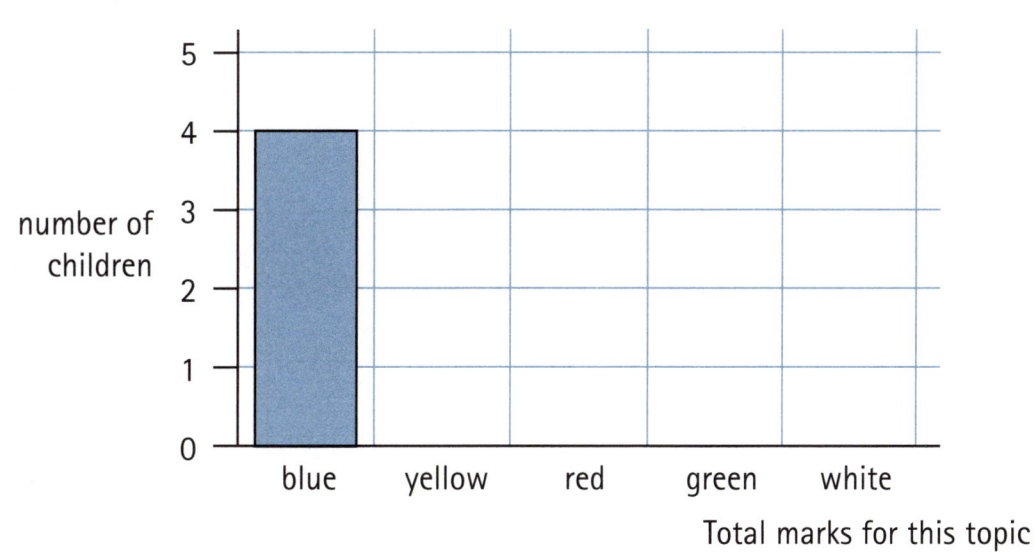

3b
2 mark

Total marks for this topic

Range and mode

1 The children at St. Jude's School collect the ring pulls from cans of drink to raise money for charity.
This table shows how many they collected during the year.

January	220
February	350
March	325
April	120
May	400
June	450
July	460
August	0
September	345
October	290
November	160
December	220

a) What is the range for the number of ring pulls collected?

b) What is the mode of the number of ring pulls collected?

c) No ring pulls were collected in August.
Why do you think this was?

HANDLING DATA 41

2) This list shows the number of minutes each bus was late arriving at a bus stop:

3   8   9   4   12   2   5   6   10   9

a) What is the mode of these times?

2a 1 mark

b) What is the range of these times?

2b 1 mark

3) Twenty children were asked for their shoe sizes.

8   6   7   6   5   4   7   6   8   10   7   5   5
8   9   7   5   6   8   6

a) What is the mode of the shoe sizes?

3a 1 mark

b) What is the range of the shoe sizes?

3b 1 mark

Total marks for this topic

Grouping data

1 Here is a list of the number of goals scored by the end of January by the teams in a football league.

32 28 14 8 15 22 22 24 39 20

20 24 26 25 23 21 14 35 26 19

Kevin puts the numbers in groups in a table.

a) Fill in the missing numbers in the table.

number of goals	1-5	6-10	11-15	16-20	21-25	26-30	31-35	36-40
number of teams	0	1	3		7			1

b) Use the table to complete the bar chart.

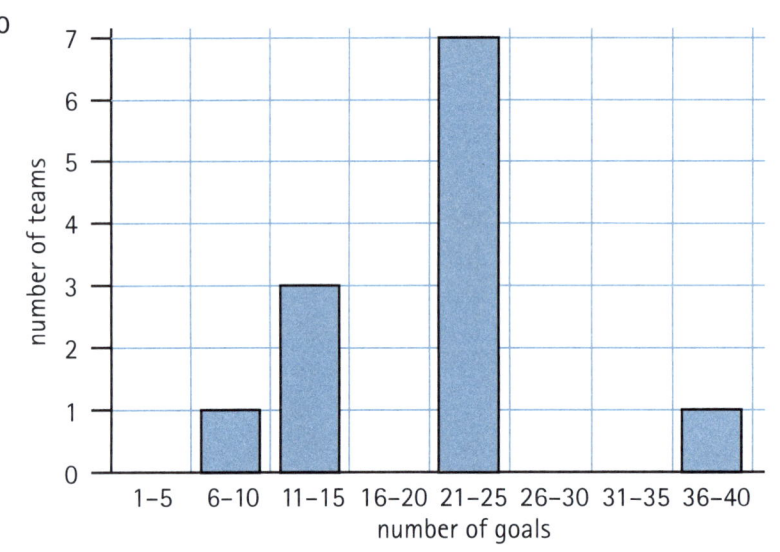

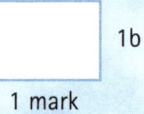

2 This bar chart shows the number of pets owned by the children in class 7.

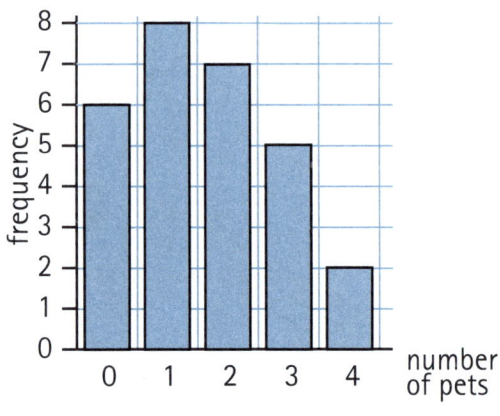

a) How many children have 3 pets?

b) All the children in class 7 took part.

How many children was this?

HANDLING DATA 43

3 Some children counted the number of people going into a library every day between 9 am and 2 pm for one week.

	9 am–10 am	10 am–11 am	11 am–12 noon	12 noon–1 pm	1 pm–2 pm
Monday	15	26	12	32	8
Tuesday	16	39	63	21	36
Wednesday	29	36	56	18	43
Thursday	31	40	44	31	26
Friday	46	49	58	38	20
Saturday	38	25	37	29	19

Complete the frequency table. Some of the entries have been done for you.

Number of people	Frequency	Total
0–9		
10–19		
20–29	|||| ||	7
30–39		
40–49	||||	5
50–59		
60–69		

2 marks

4 Amy asked some people about their favourite fruits. This bar chart shows how they answered.

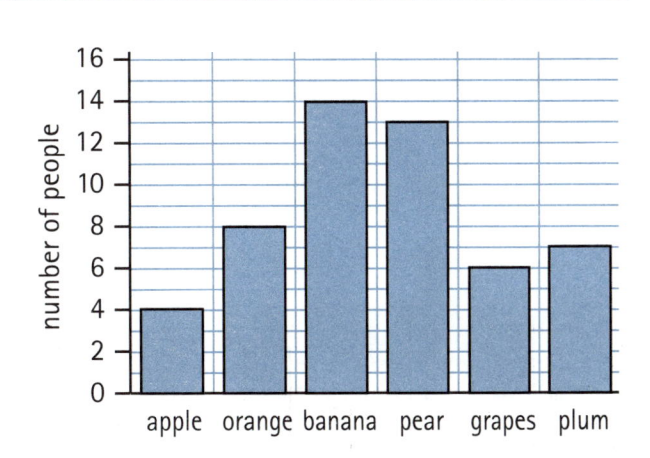

Answer these questions:

a) How many people chose pears?

1 mark

b) Which fruit was chosen by the fewest people?

1 mark

c) How many people did Amy ask?

2 marks

Total marks for this topic

Line graphs

1 Lucy was ill in April.
This is her temperature chart.

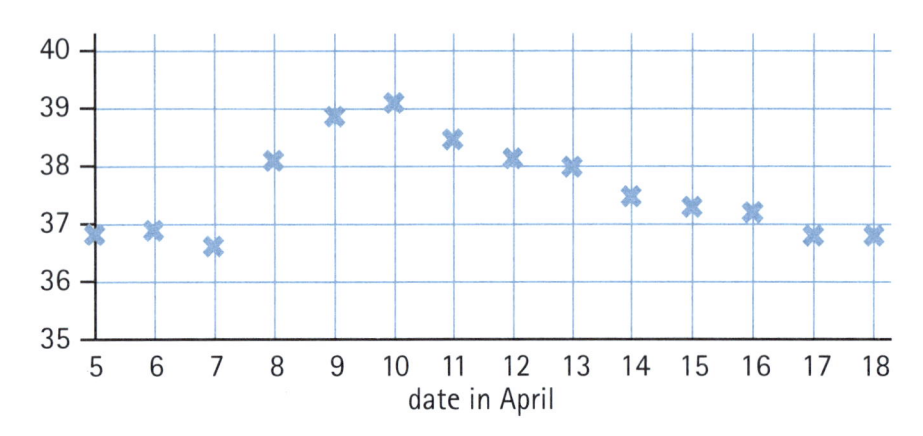

a) For how many days was Lucy's temperature more than 37 °C?

1a 1 mark

b) Estimate Lucy's highest temperature shown on the graph.
Give your answer to 1 decimal place.

☐ °C

1b 1 mark

2 These two graphs show the rainfall reading and the temperature reading during one week.

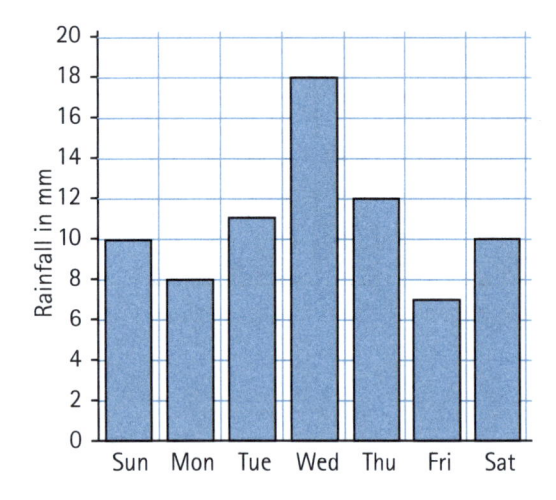

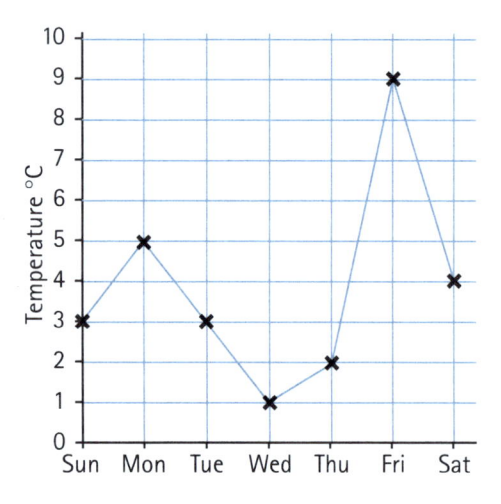

a) Use both graphs to describe what the weather was like on Wednesday.

2a 2 marks

b) Use both graphs to compare the weather on Wednesday and Friday.

2b 2 marks

3 Asif measured the length of a shadow every 30 minutes during the day and made a graph to show how the length changed.

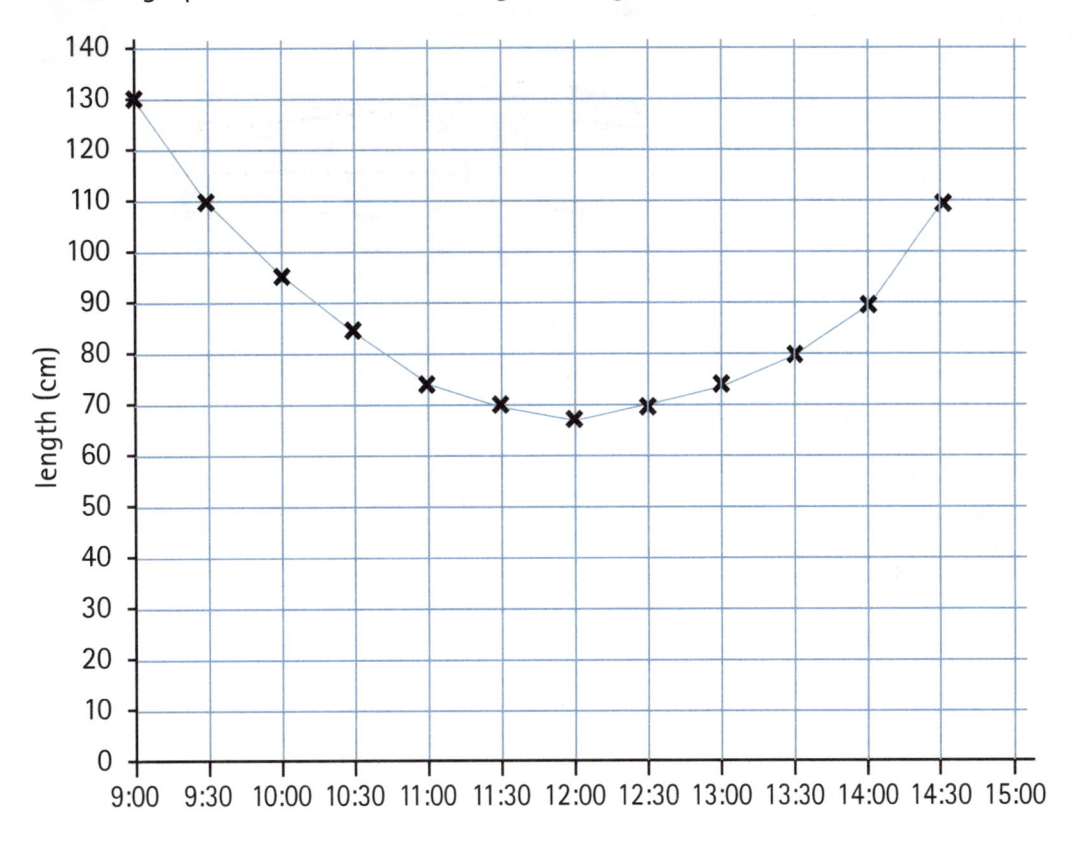

a) When was the shadow the longest?

b) When was the shadow the shortest?

c) Write down two times when the shadow length was the same.

d) What do you think the shadow length might be at 15:00?

Total marks for this topic

Problem solving 1

1 This bus has numbered seats. Here is a plan of the bus. The first few seat numbers are given.

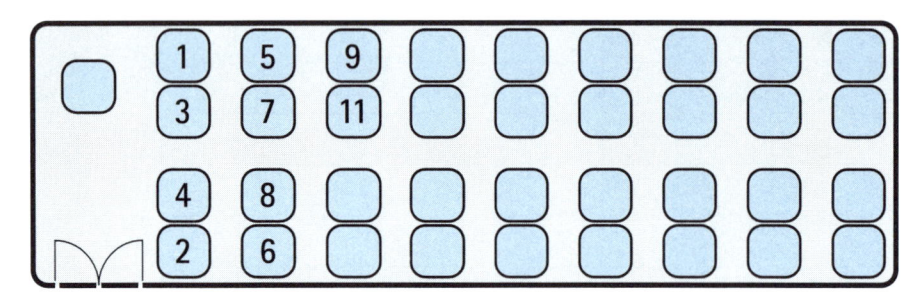

Look for a pattern in the numbers.

a) Is 30 a window seat?
Show your method.

1a — 1 mark

b) Will the children in seats 33 and 34 be sitting next to each other?
Show your method.

1b — 1 mark

2 a) Write in the missing numbers in the last triangle to continue the pattern.

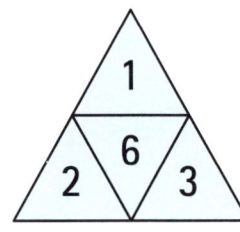

2a — 1 mark

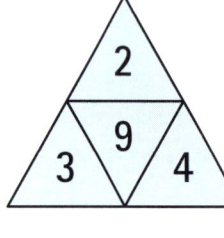

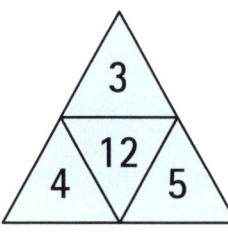

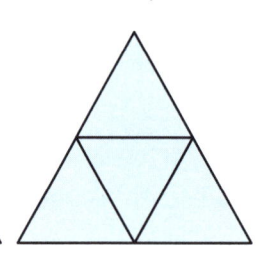

b) Explain how you worked out the missing numbers.

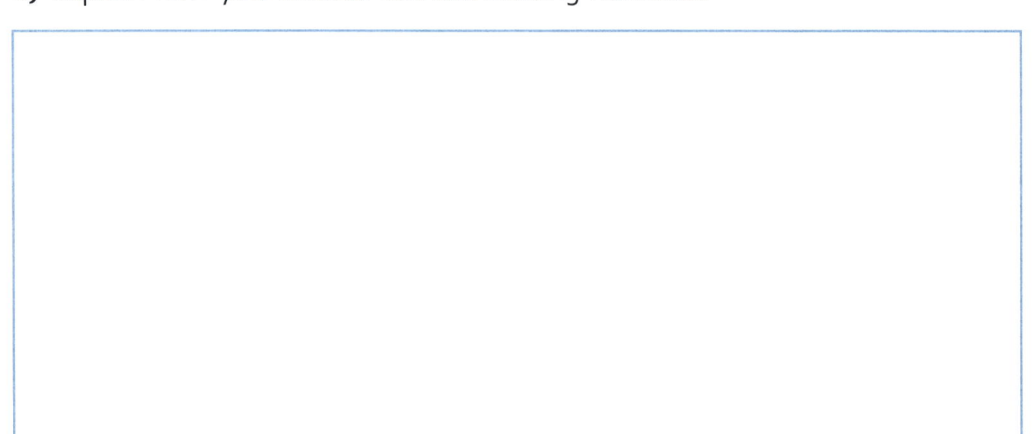

2b — 2 marks

You could write letters in the spaces like this:

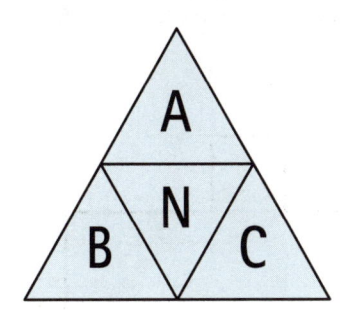

Then the rule is

'You find out what N is by adding A, B and C together.'

c) Write this rule just using the letters N, A, B and C.

3) Here is a graph.

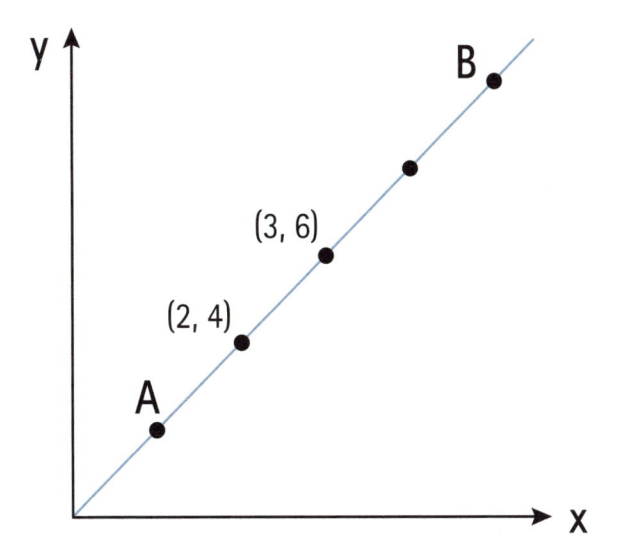

The dots (•) on the line are equally spaced.

a) What are the coordinates of the point A? (,)

Toni says:

'The point B has coordinates (5, 11).'

b) Use the graph to explain why she cannot be correct.

48 USING AND APPLYING MATHEMATICS

4 This diagram shows two shapes drawn on a centimetre square grid.

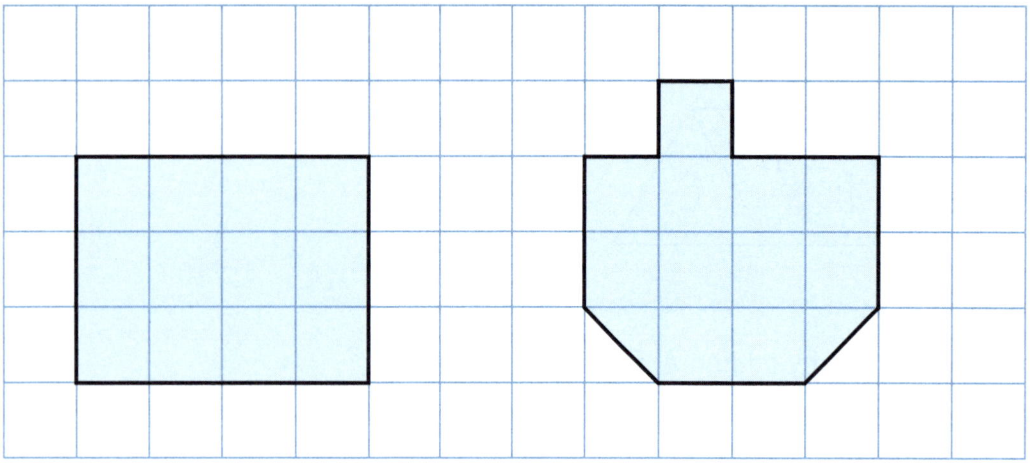

a) Do the shapes have the same area?
Tick (✔) Yes or No.   Yes ☐   No ☐

4a 1 mark

b) Explain how you know.

4b 1 mark

The perimeter of the rectangle is 14 cm.
Ben thinks the perimeter of the other shape will also be 14 cm.
c) Explain why Ben is wrong.

4c 1 mark

5 Nisha makes a sequence of 5 numbers.
The first number is 4.
The last number is 20.
Her rule is to add the same amount each time.

a) Write in the missing numbers.

| 4 | | | | 20 |

5a 1 mark

b) Show how you worked out what the numbers should be.

5b 1 mark

6 I am thinking of a whole number.

Twice my number is more than 70 and less than 80.

My number is a multiple of 3.

What could my number be?

[ ] 6

1 mark

7 ▲ ✳ and ◆ all stand for different whole numbers.

▲ + ✳ + ◆ = 13

✳ + ✳ + ▲ = 11

▲ + ▲ = 6

Find the value of each shape.

a) ▲ = [ ]   b) ✳ = [ ]   c) ◆ = [ ]

[ ] 7a
1 mark

[ ] 7b
1 mark

[ ] 7c
1 mark

8 Two numbers, A and B, add to 100.

That means   A + B = 100

The difference between them is 28.

That means   A − B = 28

What are the values of A and B?

A = [ ]   B = [ ]

[ ] 8
2 marks

Total marks for this topic [ ]

Problem solving 2

1 Here is a 'Think of a number' puzzle.
Follow the instructions in turn.
Write your answer in the box at the end of each line.

Think of a whole number between 1 and 4.

Double your number.

Add 3 to your last number.

Double your last number.

Add 2 to the last number.

Divide the very last number by 4.

Take away the number you started with.

Is your answer 2? Write in yes or no.

1 mark

2 On sports day the children in Albany School get points for each event they take part in. This table shows the points they get depending on how far they jump.

Standing Long Jump	
over 80 cm	1 point
over 100 cm	2 points
over 120 cm	3 points
over 140 cm	4 points
over 160 cm	5 points
over 180 cm	6 points

a) Tom jumped 138 cm.
How many points did he get?

2a
1 mark

b) Harry said 'I jumped 1.5 metres. I get 4 points'
Give a reason why Harry is correct.

2b
1 mark

3 127 children visit a museum.
They go in groups of 15. One group has less than 15 children.
Every group of children has one adult with them.

a) How many adults will need to go?
   Show your method.

3a 1 mark

Mrs Hunter buys 7 drinks at 64p each and 8 drinks at 72p each.

b) What is the total cost of the drinks?
   Show your method.

3b 1 mark

4 Tom and Mary went to the fair. They both had £10.00 to spend.

Big Dipper £2.25   *Waltzer £1.50*

Ghost Train £2.50

Roundabout £1.80   *Big Wheel £1.75*

a) Mary had a ride on each.
   How much did this cost?

4a 1 mark

b) Tom had 2 rides on the Big Dipper and 2 rides on the Waltzer.
   Did he have enough money to ride on the Ghost Train?
   Show your method.

4b 1 mark

52 USING AND APPLYING MATHEMATICS

5 Here are some picture frame sizes.

height in cm	10	12	14	16
length in cm	16	20	24	28

For each frame, the length, (L), is twice the height, (H), subtract 4.

a) What is the length of a frame which has a height of 36 cm?
Show your method.

5a
2 marks

b) Write the rule in symbols.

5b
2 marks

c) A new frame has its length twice its height.
It is made from 126 cm of wood.
What is the length of this frame?
Show your method.

5c
2 marks

6

1st
```
    1
  4 ○ 2
    3
```

2nd
```
    2
  5 ○ 3
    4
```

3rd
```
    3
  6 ○ 4
    5
```

The number in the circle in each shape is found by adding the numbers in the four squares.

a) Write the numbers in the circles for the first three shapes.

6a
1 mark

b) What number will go in the top square of the 6th shape?

6b
1 mark

Look at the numbers in the first two shapes:

1st shape
1 + 4 = 5, 2 + 3 = 5 and 5 + 5 = 10, which is the number in the circle.

2nd shape
2 + 5 = 7, 3 + 4 = 7 and 7 + 7 = 14, which is the number in the circle.

c) The number in a circle is 34.
Use this pattern to work out what the numbers in the squares must be.

6c

2 marks

7 Two pints of milk cost 62p.
What is the cost of 5 pints of milk at the same price per pint?
Show your method.

7

2 marks

8 This shaded shape is made by joining dots on a centimetre squared grid.

What is its area?
Show how you worked it out.

8

2 marks

Total marks for this topic

Level 4 Sample Test

1) Write what the four missing digits could be.

☐☐☐ ÷ 10 = 3☐

1 mark

2) a) Write what the two missing numbers could be.

☐ ÷ ☐ = 8

1 mark

b) Write what the two missing numbers could be.

(6 + ☐) × ☐ = 100

1 mark

c) Write what the missing number is.

30 − 17 = 8 + ☐

1 mark

3) Write two numbers, each greater than 100, to complete this subtraction.

☐☐☐ − ☐☐☐ = 208

1 mark

4) Some children at Lakeside School ran a race. Here are their times.

Name	Time in seconds
Joanne	23.4
Zahid	21.8
Andrea	19.5
Nick	18.7
Sonja	20.8
Simon	24.2
Theresa	22.2
Julia	24.9
Andrew	19.6
Paul	19.9

a) Who was the fastest runner?

1 mark

b) What was the range of the times?

1 mark

5 Write these percentages in the correct boxes.

20%   50%   9%   30%   40%   75%   60%

Less than a half	A half	More than a half

2 marks

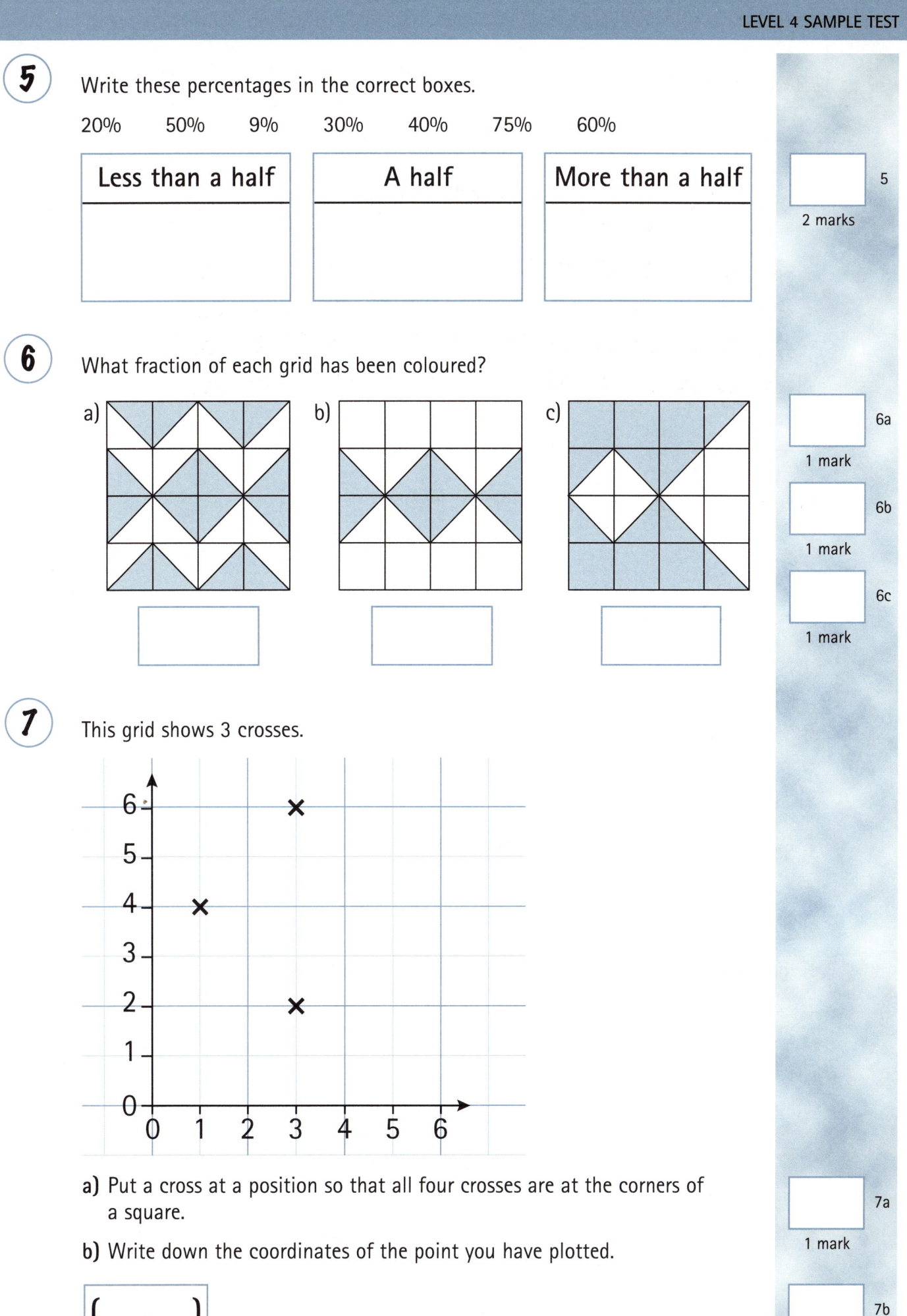

6 What fraction of each grid has been coloured?

a)   b)   c)

1 mark (6a)
1 mark (6b)
1 mark (6c)

7 This grid shows 3 crosses.

a) Put a cross at a position so that all four crosses are at the corners of a square.

b) Write down the coordinates of the point you have plotted.

(,   )

1 mark (7a)
2 marks (7b)

8 Look at this calendar.

JULY						
Mon	Tue	Wed	Thu	Fri	Sat	Sun
			1	2	3	4
5	6	7	8	9	10	11
12	13	14	15	16	17	18
19	20	21	22	23	24	25
26	27	28	29	30	31	

AUGUST						
Mon	Tue	Wed	Thu	Fri	Sat	Sun
						1
2	3	4	5	6	7	8
9	10	11	12	13	14	15
16	17	18	19	20	21	22
23	24	25	26	27	28	29
30	31					

a) What was the date of the third Tuesday in July?

b) How many Sundays were there in August?

c) School sports day was on July 9th. What day was this?

d) School finished two weeks later. What was the date?

e) In August what day had numbers in the 7 times table as its dates?

9 Look at these shapes drawn on a square grid.

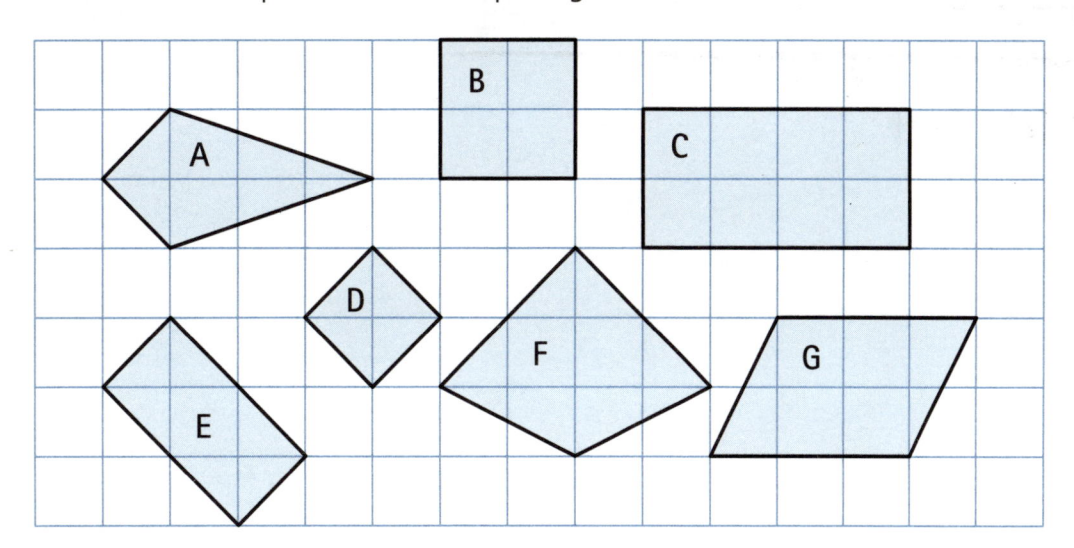

Fill in the table which sorts the shapes into groups.
Tick (✔) the box if the description fits.

Shape	All sides equal	Opposite sides parallel	All angles right angles
A			
B			
C			
D			
E			
F			
G			

2 marks

10 Harry is packing cubes into a box.

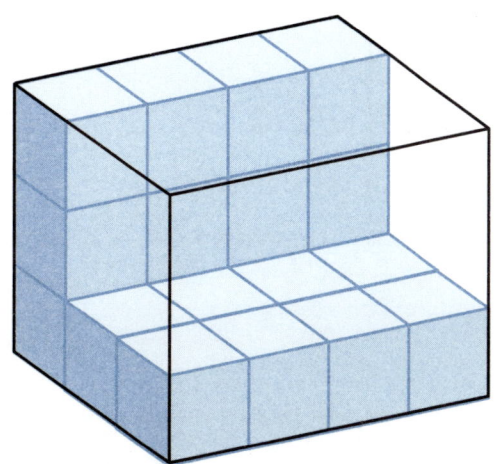

He has filled the base and one side.
How many cubes will the box hold when it is full?

1 mark

Total marks for the test /23

Answers

Level 3 Sample Test

1. **a)** −2°C
   b) −7°C
   c) 5°C

2. **a)** 71   109   146   189   220   247
   b) 176
   c) 184

3. 4
   1

4. eg 75 and 65, or 74 and 66, or 73 and 67 etc

5. 75 90 95 all circled

6. **a)** 6
   b) 3

7. 16 × 20 = 320 ringed

8. **a)** A   C   E
   b) F   D
   c) B

9. **a)** Ann 40, Paul 25, David 20, Jane 15
   b) for Robert – clear representation of 35 comics

10. $\frac{2}{8}$ and $\frac{1}{4}$ linked

11. check 6 squares shaded

    eg $\frac{6}{12}$

    eg $\frac{1}{2}$

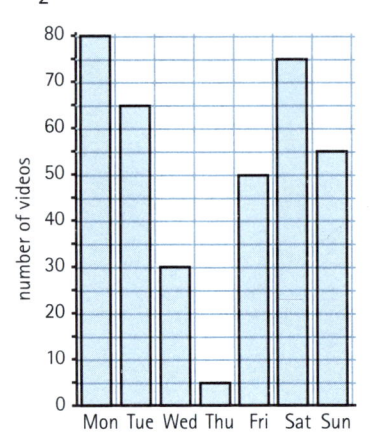

12. [bar chart: number of videos — Mon 80, Tue 65, Wed 30, Thu 5, Fri 50, Sat 75, Sun 55]

Place value

1 Numbers circled: 20 30 6 4 26 2
   Numbers crossed: 20 30 25 45

2 19
   6
   228

3 a) 357
   b) 3570
   c) 753
   d) 251

4
÷	2	3	6
30	15	10	5
48	24	16	8
18	9	6	3

5 a) 17 tens ringed
   b) 1200

6 7

Addition and subtraction

1 a) Check working, eg 462 and 538
   b) Check working, eg 1144 and 856
   c) Check working, eg 2646 and 2354

2 6
   2

3
```
    2 5 8
  + 2 9 7
    -----
    5 5 5
```

4 7

5 82
   but 518 seen with incorrect answer award 1 mark

6 Diagram: 15 → 150, 15 → 30, 3 → 30, 3 → 150

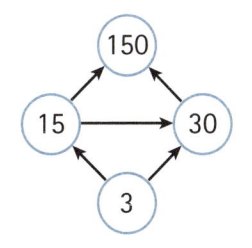

Decimals

1 a) 6
   b) Kathy
   c) 2.9 seconds

2 £40.75

3 5.15

4
   1.39 + 3.21 → 4.60
   3.21 − 1.10 → 2.11
   6.01 + 3.10 → 9.11
   9.01 − 8.75 → 0.26
   6.88 − 5.19 → 1.69
   8.80 + 1.19 → 9.99

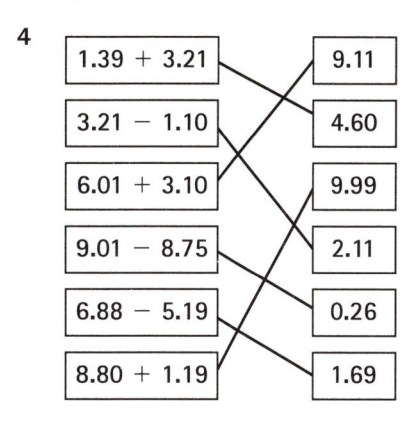

5 a) 6.01, 6.00, 5.99
   b) 0.621, 0.64, 1.35, 1.85, 2.26, 2.9

Finding reasonable answers

1 a) £9.90
   b) £10.40
   c) £2.60
   d) eg £2.60 × 4 seen, or £10 ÷ 4 = £2.50, 40p ÷ 4 = 10p

2 a) 2826
   b) 2826 ÷ 18 = 157, or 20 × 160 = 3200 therefore a bit less

3 a) 15
   b) 5
   c) 6

4 4

5 a) £3.67
   b) 12

6 a) eg because the flour weighs 1500 g
   b) 2.720 kg or 2720 g

ANSWERS

Proportions, fractions and percentages

1. a) £1.00
   b) £3.60
   c) 600 ml
2. a) $\frac{3}{8}$
   b) $\frac{10}{16} = \frac{5}{8}$
3. a) $\frac{40}{60} = \frac{2}{3}$
   b) 15
4. a) eg $\frac{3}{6}$
   b) eg $\frac{5}{15}$
5. Less than a half: $\frac{1}{10}$ $\frac{1}{20}$ $\frac{1}{100}$ $\frac{2}{8}$ $\frac{1}{3}$
   A half: $\frac{4}{8}$ $\frac{25}{50}$
   More than a half: $\frac{6}{10}$ $\frac{60}{100}$ $\frac{3}{5}$

Number patterns

1. a) 2+4+6+8 (shown on grid)
   b) 2 →+4→ 6 →+6→ 12 →+8→ 20 →+10→ 30 →+12→ 42
2. a) 2, 6, 5, 9, 8, 12, 11, 15, 14, 18
   b) eg "They go up in threes"
3. a) −2
   b) 243 and 1
4. a) 9
   b) 6
5. a) 4 is a Factor of 20
   b) 5 is a Factor of 35 and 65
   c) 36 is a Square number
   d) 3 is a Prime number; it is also a Factor of 12
   e) 25 is a Multiple of 5
   f) The first four Prime numbers are 2, 3, 5, 7

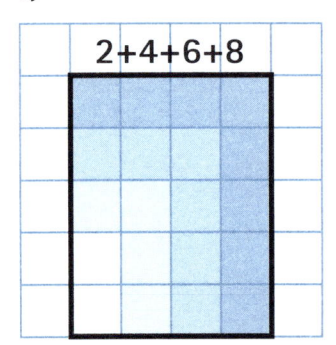

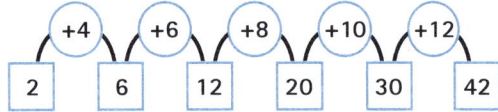

Simple formulae

1. £63
2. 25 mph
3. 18.5 m
4. a) 192
   b) 3
5. | time in hours | cost in £ |
   |---|---|
   | 1 | 5 |
   | 4 | 14 |
   | 5 | 17 |
6. a) 14
   b) 8

Coordinates

1 **a)** Insert (4,3) and (5,2)
   b) (1,6) (2,5) (3,4) (4,3) (5,2) (6,1)
   c) eg the first number goes up by 1 and the second number goes down by 1
   eg the sum of each pair = 7

2 **a)** check drawing, cross at (3, 3)
   b) (3, 3)

2D and 3D shapes

1 **a)** Cube = C; **b)** Cuboid = A; **c)** Cylinder = E
   d) Triangular prism = D **e)** Square-based pyramid = B

2 **a)** 11
   b)

3 eg

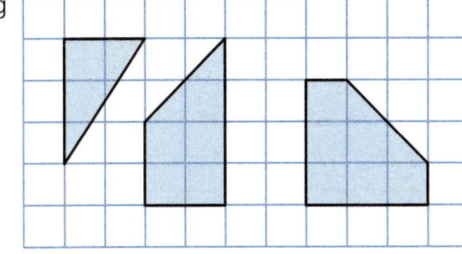

4 **a)** B, D
   b) D

Reflection

1

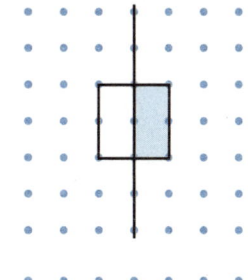

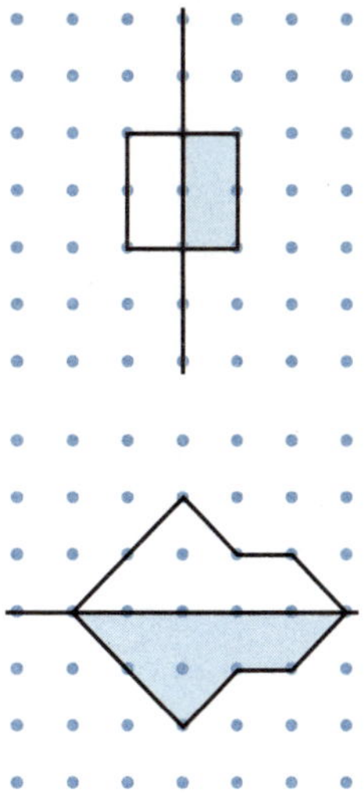

2

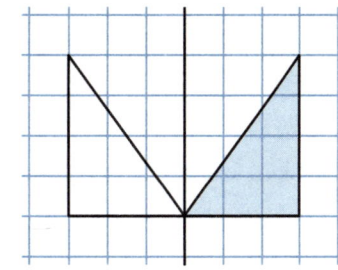

3 **a)**

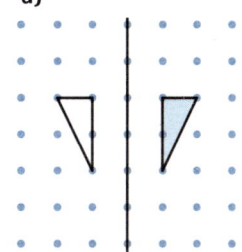

   b)

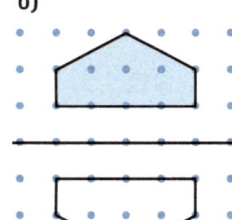

�# Measures

1. 7.8 cm
2. a) A = 9.8 cm
   b) B = 10.8 cm
   c) C = 13 cm
3. a) 0.25 litres
   b) 20 cm long
   c) 100 g
4. About 73 kg, accept an answer greater than 70 and less than 75
5. 250 indicated
6. 700 ml

Perimeter and area

1. a) Area = 19 sq cm perimeter = 20 cm
   b) Area = 13 sq cm perimeter = 16 cm
2. a) Check drawing
   b) Check drawing
3. a) Area = 5 sq cm
   b) $\frac{5}{25}$ or $\frac{1}{5}$

Frequency tables

1. a)
Number of children	Tally	Total
1	++++ ++++	10
2	++++ ++++ //	12
3	////	4
4	/	1

   b) Bar chart: number of families vs number of children in family (1→10, 2→12, 3→4, 4→1)

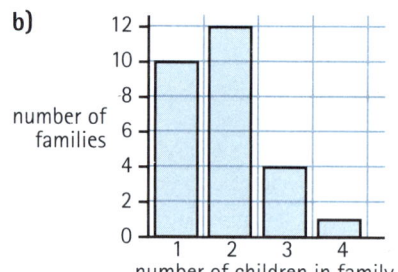

2. a)
Shoe size	Tally	Total
4	/	1
5	++++ ///	8
6	++++ ++++	10
7	++++ ///	8
8	///	3

   b) Bar chart: number of children vs shoe size (4→1, 5→8, 6→10, 7→8, 8→3)

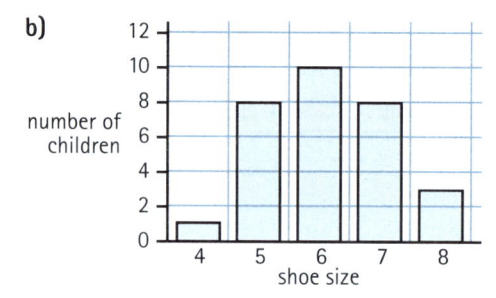

3. a)
Colour	Tally	Frequency
blue	////	4
yellow	///	3
red	////	4
green	///	3
white	//	2

   b) Bar chart: number of children (blue→4, yellow→3, red→4, green→3, white→2)

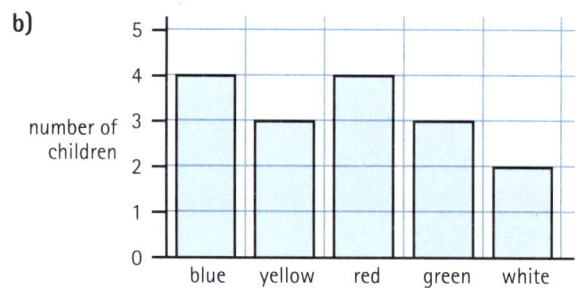

Range and mode

1. a) Range = 460
   b) Mode = 220
   c) School holiday

2. a) Mode = 9 minutes
   b) Range = 10 minutes

3. a) Mode = size 6
   b) Range = 6

Grouping data

1. a)

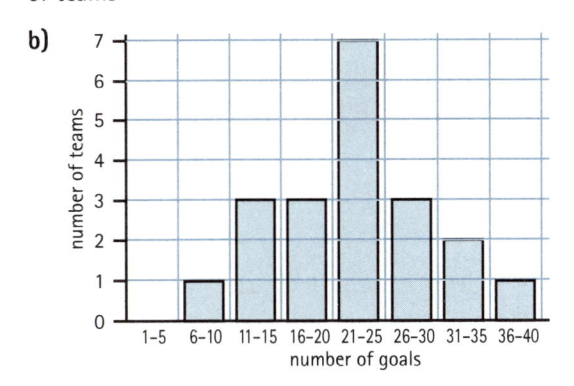

number of goals	1-5	6-10	11-15	16-20	21-25	26-30	31-35	36-40
number of teams	0	1	3	3	7	3	2	1

   b) [bar chart of number of teams vs number of goals]

2. a) 5
   b) 6 + 8 + 7 + 5 + 2 = 28

3.
Number of people	Frequency	Total
0–9	/	1
10–19	////	5
20–29	//// //	7
30–39	//// ////	9
40–49	////	5
50–59	//	2
60–69	/	1

4. a) 13
   b) Apple
   c) 4+8+14+13+6+7 = 52

Line graphs

1. a) 9
   b) 39.2°C Accept 39.1 to 39.3

2. a) eg wet and cold
   b) Friday was hotter and drier than Wednesday

3. a) 0900
   b) 1200
   c) eg 0930 and 1430
   d) 130 cm

Problem solving 1

1. a) Yes. Number sequence goes up in 4's,
      2, 6, 10, 14, 18, 22, 26, 30
   b) No, 34 is in one sequence, 33 is in different sequence

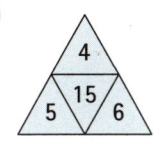

2. a) [triangle with 4 at top, 5 bottom-left, 6 bottom-right, 15 in middle]
   b) eg The top number, bottom left and bottom right numbers all go up by 1 each time. The middle number goes up by 3.
   c) N = A + B + C

3. a) (1, 2)
   b) Because the 2nd number, (the y coordinate), is double the 1st number, (the x-coordinate)

4. a) Yes b) eg counted squares
   c) eg because the diagonal lines are longer than the sides of a square

5. a) 4 8 12 16 20
   b) eg the first number is 4, the 5th number is 20
      20 is 5 × 4, so numbers go up in 4's
      eg by trial and improvement

6. 36 or 39

7. a) ▲ = 3
   b) ✳ = 4
   c) ◆ = 6

8. A = 64   B = 36

Problem solving 2

1. 2 but check working
2. **a)** 3 points
   b) eg because 1.5 metres = 150 cm which is between 140cm and 160cm
3. **a)** eg 127 ÷ 15 = 8 r7, therefore 9 adults
   b) 7 × 64 = £4.48   8 × 72 = £5.72
   £4.48 + £5.76 = £10.24
4. **a)** £9.80
   b) yes, £10.00 - £7.50 = £2.50
5. **a)** eg 2 × 36 = 72
   72 - 4 = 68cm
   b) L = 2H - 4
   c) 2H + H + 2H + H = 126
   6H = 126
   H = 21 therefore L = 42
6. **a)** 10, 14, 18
   b) 6
   c) 7, 8, 9, 10
7. 1 costs 31p
   5 cost 5 × 31 = £1. 55
8. eg

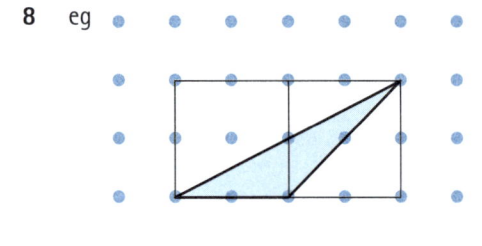

   dividing into large rectangle , 4 × 2, and 'removing' half leaving area of 4
   dividing into small square and removing half leaving 2
   therefore area remaining = 4 - 2 = 2

Level 4 Sample Test

1. eg $\boxed{3}\boxed{4}\boxed{0}$ ÷ 10 = $\boxed{3}\boxed{4}$
   1st number must be 3, the 2nd numbers must correspond, the 3rd number is zero
2. **a)** eg $\boxed{16}$ ÷ $\boxed{2}$ = 8
   b) (6 + $\boxed{4}$) × $\boxed{10}$ = 100
   c) 30 − 17 = 8 + $\boxed{5}$
3. eg $\boxed{3}\boxed{0}\boxed{9}$ − $\boxed{1}\boxed{0}\boxed{1}$ = 208
4. **a)** Nick
   b) range = 24.9 - 18.7 = 6.2 secs
5. Less than a half   A half   More than a half
   20% 9% 30% 40%   50%   60% 75%
6. **a)** $\frac{1}{2}$
   b) $\frac{1}{4}$
   c) $\frac{10}{16}$ or $\frac{5}{8}$
7. **a)** correctly plotted at (5, 4)
   b) (5, 4)
8. **a)** 20th
   b) 5
   c) Friday
   d) 23rd July
   e) Saturday
9.
Shape	All sides equal	Opposite sides parallel	All angles right angles
A			
B	✔	✔	✔
C		✔	✔
D	✔	✔	✔
E		✔	✔
F			
G		✔	

10. 36